Aids to Reading

Aids to Reading

John M. Hughes

Evans Brothers Limited, London

Published by Evans Brothers Limited
Montague House, Russell Square, London W.C.1

© John M. Hughes 1970
First published 1970
Reprinted 1971
Reprinted 1972

Printed Offset Litho in Great Britain by Cox & Wyman Ltd., London, Fakenham and Reading.

237 28381 6   PRA 2682

Contents

Acknowledgements

The author and publishers would like to thank Holmes McDougall Ltd for permission to reproduce material from the *Manual for the Programmed Reading Kit* by D. H. Stott; Thomas Nelson & Sons Ltd for the material from *Mr Nen and his friends, Part I*; Stillit Books Ltd for the material from *Programmed Remedial Reading Texts, Book 1*, by S. Bhattacharya, and for the photograph of the Stillitron; Frederick Warne & Co Ltd for permission to reproduce pages 16 and 17 from *The Tale of Benjamin Bunny* (i.t.a. edition) by Beatrix Potter; and *Teacher's World*, where much of the material in Chapter 2 first appeared.

They are also grateful to Bell & Howell Ltd for the photograph of the Language Master; to the Educational Supply Association Ltd for the photographs of the Canterbury Mark II Teaching Machine and of the Esatutor; and to Science Research Associates Limited for the photographs of the SRA Reading Laboratories.

Artwork by George Craig
Cover photograph by Henry Grant

Introduction

'If children are to become capable of realizing their potential in later life, they must acquire the basic tools that a twentieth-century society demands. We have failed if a group of children leave school without any real knowledge of how to understand and handle these tools. If a child leaves school unable to read or inhibited from reading because of continuous difficulties, he suffers a communication handicap which will sharply affect his choice of career, his earning capacity, and his role as a member of a society whose daily bread is the printed word.'[1]

There is an abundance of literature on the teaching of reading, but the majority of books and articles are primarily concerned with the theory of teaching reading, and, frequently, with the statistical justification for the adoption of a specific method. Teachers are able to peruse ample literature on the main methods of teaching reading and most know that these are the alphabetic, phonic, 'look and say', 'whole word' and sentence methods. These teachers may appreciate the importance, values and aims of each method. They probably appreciate that the alphabetic method places emphasis on the names and shapes of letters and that this probably helps in learning letter sequences and left to right word attack; that this method may help spelling ability. They probably realise that the phonic

[1] *The Challenge of Reading Failure*. N.F.E.R, 1968, p. 41.

method helps the child to recognise shapes of letters and word parts and that its greatest advantage is in 'unlocking' unfamiliar words. They are probably well aware that the 'look and say' and 'whole word' method emphasises the patterns of words and that pictures may help the child in learning meaningful words; that this particular method helps the child to learn those words that are phonically irregular. They probably know that the sentence method emphasises the sentence as the unit of meaning and that its main advantage is in helping fluent reading.

However, teachers of reading need help in dealing with those children who are having difficulty with reading. They wish to know what they can do for these children. They want practical advice, specific suggestions for things to do in reading, advice and suggestions on the various reading materials, games and activities, advice on the various published Reading Programmes and other media, advice and suggestions concerning the use of audio-visual aids and the use and value of teaching machines. Above all, they want someone to talk to them in practical terms.

I have found that, on many occasions, when visiting schools, a child's reading ability is judged on the progress which he has made in a particular reading scheme. When I have given the child reading books or reading material of comparable difficulty, I have frequently found that the child's reading ability falls dramatically. It has become quite apparent to me that if a child is confined to the narrowness of one reading scheme without the opportunity of other varied reading experiences, then this is harmful to the child's growth and independence in reading.

Aids to Reading is based on my experiences as a remedial teacher of reading and is the outcome of the work which I have carried out in the classroom and with remedial groups.

First, I discuss briefly the prevailing problem and how, in my opinion, local education authorities, Colleges of Education and teachers may all help to alleviate the problem of reading failure. Secondly, I discuss the use of reading games and activities which I have found effective in helping the child along the 'reading road' and it is hoped that these will encourage the teacher of reading to adopt further innovations. Thirdly, I discuss Programmed Learning and the use and value of a published Programmed Reading Kit. Fourthly, I consider the use of a selection of teaching machines and place particular emphasis on my experiments with the tape recorder. Finally, I discuss a few other reading aids and media which many teachers may wish to use with their children.

The games, activities, materials, aids and other media discussed, involve either a specific method or a combination of two or more. I do not discuss the arguments for and against a particular method of teaching reading. An enormous amount of research on the teaching of reading has indicated that no single method is superior to all others. What is more important is that the teacher believes in and is enthusiastic about the method(s) he or she is using. I do not suggest that the use of one Reading Programme, one teaching machine or one of many other media may be the panacea for all reading ills, but my attitude is that I am prepared to use anything which may help a child, in some way or other, along the 'reading road'.

Finally, I would emphasise that even though there is a tremendous amount of value in discovery methods and incidental learning, the teaching of reading should not be left solely to this approach. During my work as a remedial teacher, it became very apparent to me that most children will not learn the skills of reading if left completely to their own devices. Frequently, I have been asked to help children experiencing reading difficulties who have required systematic teaching based on their individual needs. Therefore, teachers must appreciate that children, generally, must be *taught* to read and that all aids to reading are complementary to the teaching.

1

The problem

Reading skill is a complex of abilities and includes visual perception and discrimination, auditory perception and discrimination, association of visual and auditory patterns, linguistic ability and a capacity for the detailed analysis of the sound structure of individual words. Reading is a skill of paramount importance. It may be regarded as a 'tool' skill in the sense that it affects most aspects of children's learning in school and a child's progress in other subjects will depend considerably on his reading ability. The acquisition of reading ability opens many doors and reading failure is, therefore, a major factor in educational failure. Reading failure can affect a child's whole attitude to school and, in some cases, engender emotional disturbance.

There appears to be little doubt that reading attainments have improved over the last ten years.[1, 2] Many local education authorities and teachers have put in tremendous efforts to tackle the problem of backwardness in reading. There has been a growth of special schools, special classes, reading clinics, remedial teachers, full-time courses and in-service courses for teachers. We must not, however, become complacent because there are still too many children with reading attainments which are inadequate. There exists a considerable number of

[1] *Progress in Reading*, Educ. Pamph., No. 50, H.M.S.O., 1966.
[2] Plowden Report, Vol. 2, p. 428–433, H.M.S.O., 1967.

children who are either failing to learn to read, or are mastering only the bare mechanics.

The findings of 13 years' research into reading standards and progress in a group of primary schools in Kent by Dr. Joyce Morris[1] showed that one out of eight children is unable to read by the age of eight. She found that half of these remained semi-literate until the end of their school days with a resulting occupational handicap which must still be affecting their lives.

The most serious defect that Dr Morris emphasised was the inability of first-year junior teachers to diagnose reading backwardness accurately and provide a remedy. Almost half the children reaching junior school still needed infant teaching, but only one junior teacher out of four had received training in infant method. She also found that teachers in half of the junior schools did not use reading apparatus at all because they believed that children considered it 'babyish'.

Adequate reading provision for children in the first year of the junior school should be regarded as fundamental to their whole future. If action is not taken at this time, or before then, future progress will be adversely affected.

There have been many heated arguments over the suggestion that reading may be taught before primary school age. Many educationists state that a child will not normally be ready to learn to read until he has a mental age of at least six years, and they suggest that it is extremely dangerous to attempt to accelerate the process because this will interfere with emotional and intellectual development. Many emphasise that children are not ready for specific instruction in reading until a certain level of maturity has been reached.[2, 3, 4] There

[1] Morris, J., *Standards and Progress in Reading*, N.F.E.R., 1966.

[2] Schonell, F. J., *The Psychology and Teaching of Reading*, Oliver & Boyd, Edinburgh, 1961.

[3] Malmquist, E., *Factors Related to Reading Disabilities in the First Grade of the Elementary School*, Almqvist & Wiksell, Stockholm, 1958.

[4] Sampson, O. C., 'Reading skill at eight years in relation to speech and other factors', *Brit. J. Educ. Psychol.*, **32**, 12–17, 1962.

is a growing body of opinion, however, which suggests that these dangers are overstated.[1, 2, 3] I would suggest that if a child learns to read early then he will gain a lasting advantage not only in reading skill but in a far wider sphere of intellectual progress. This advantage is especially important for the slow learning child.

Early ascertainment

Local education authorities can do more to tackle the problem of reading failure. The prevailing restriction of nursery schools means that many children, who require the stimulation which is lacking at home, are still being neglected. Early ascertainment is required in order that teachers become aware of children who may be regarded as 'educational risks' as early as possible in their schooling. In order to carry this out, it would become necessary to ascertain a child's capacities during pre-school years. It is appreciated that the earlier a child is examined, the more difficult is the accurate assessment of his potential, but this does not mean that, in many cases, we should wait for a child to fail before taking action. If a child's intellectual capacity is to be ascertained before the start of his primary education, then this could be done in nursery schools. Special units could be set up in these nursery schools and priority could be given, to begin with, to 'at risk' cases (in the medical sense). This 'at risk' register could be the basis for early assessment of intellectual impairment. The nursery units could eventually alleviate the burdens of many mothers with large families who, for various reasons, are unable to give the necessary care, attention and stimulation to their children.

Many pre-school children who eventually require special educational treatment have suffered from cultural deprivation

[1] Diack, H., *Reading and the Psychology of Perception*, Ray Palmer, Nottingham, 1960.
[2] Downing, J. A., 'Is a "Mental Age of Six" essential for reading readiness?' *Educ. Res.* **6**, 16–28, 1963.
[3] Doman, G., *Teach Your Baby to Read*, Jonathan Cape, 1963.

at home. Such children could be provided with the stimulation that is missing in the home. The environment of the nursery should be such that it promotes curiosity, the spoken language and readiness for intellectual activities that will come later. The school day should include a good deal of reading to children and discussion of what has been read as well as what the children will have seen on television. After all, it is during the first four or five years of a child's life that physical and mental growth are not only the most rapid but also most susceptible to influence by environment.

The reading programme
Significant differences exist among children, both in learning rate and in learning capacity. One is able to observe a wide range of reading ability in almost every classroom. Some pupils may be at an 'average' level in vocabulary, below average in comprehension and above average in word-attack. These individual differences become more and more pronounced as children move up through the school and even in the first year infant class, pupils arrive at school with different intellectual capacities, different experiences and different rates of completing various tasks.

In a particular class, the range of reading ability may be from one and a half to two years with each additional year of primary schooling. Some children will improve very quickly, sometimes gaining two years in reading attainment for each year spent in school; whereas, slower children will do well to gain half a year during the same amount of time.

If a teacher is planning a reading programme with the individual requirements of each child in mind, then it should be remembered that growth in reading ability is never a smooth upward growth curve. Children will differ in the speed with which they are able to complete a piece of work. We are all familiar with a situation where many children in a class are waiting for the remainder to finish a piece of work. In reading, the situation is even more pronounced. Some children require more practice than others in order to attain proficiency. I suppose that in an ideal teaching situation, each child would work with his own teacher who would teach the skill at the child's individual level. In practice, however, if a teacher is confronted with 30 to 40 pupils, he seldom has time to confer with individual pupils. In the same way as text-books are geared to the average reader, so the teacher gears his approach to the average child in a reading group. This problem may be partially overcome, however, if material is so planned that pupils are allowed to progress in small, logical steps at their own pace and maximum learning may take place if the material provides the learner with an immediate indication of how he has performed. Children become frustrated if forced to conform to a pace which is either too slow or too fast and which creates attitudes that result in the rejection of the task. It is extremely important, therefore, that the teacher should keep detailed information on the progress of each individual child. Neale's *Analysis of Reading Ability*[1] is a very useful aid for diagnosing reading difficulties.

Remedial teaching

Most non-readers and backward readers in our primary schools are late starters or slow learners. These are the children who create problems for many teachers. They are usually provided for with what has become known as 'remedial teaching'. Remedial teaching is good first teaching and remedial methods are in essence the same as the methods adopted in the successful teaching of so-called normal children. They differ only in that they are applied with greater flexibility and more discrimination. Remedial methods, therefore, are based upon normal classroom practice, the things a good teacher ought to do. Teachers should have confidence in

[1] Neale, M. D., *Neale Analysis of Reading Ability*, Macmillan, London, 1958.

themselves, a sympathetic understanding of the child, an appreciation of the limitation of the child, and a precise knowledge and understanding of the reading materials available and used at different levels of ability. When working out his reading programme, the teacher should consider his own personality and his approach with the class. If the approach is good and the child can relax, then the atmosphere created will enable the child to take success and failure in his stride.

The first stage in remedial teaching is the attempt on the part of the teacher to restore in the child a desire to communicate. Reading, like any other form of communication, is a social two-way process. The second stage is for the teacher and child to discover between them areas of interest which have to be studied and enjoyed. It is essential that the teacher considers the world of the child and his fears, needs, satisfactions and hopes. It is surprising how children respond to reading material that interests them. Frequently, if materials are particularly interesting, children will reach a reading level well above what is expected.

During the last 25 years, many local education authorities have set up Remedial Education services to assist children who, while remaining within the normal school, fail to read. Many such local education authorities have expanded their Remedial Education services in such a way that more and more teachers have been appointed as peripatetic remedial teachers. These teachers visit groups of schools and provide extra tuition for small groups of children for periods varying from 25 to 35 minutes, two or three times a week. This approach, however, has its limitations because it may only bring about short-term gains and improvement may not be maintained by some children when the treatment is terminated. This point has been raised by many investigators, including Curr and Gourlay[1],

[1] Curr, W., & Gourlay N., 'The effects of practice on performance in scholastic tests', *Brit. J. Educ. Psychol.*, **30**, 2, 155–167, 1960.

Collins[1], Lovell *et al.*[2,3] and Cashdan and Pumfrey[4]. I would suggest that improvement may be very short-lived if remedial treatment consists solely of providing children with a more concentrated form of what they have experienced in the normal classroom situation and the improvement in reading is based on the result of drilling the children with words contained in the particular reading scheme(s) being used.

Remedial treatment which consists of a total approach to the child in need will help to overcome the problem of having to cater again for the child whose benefit has been short-lived. Lasting benefit can only be derived from remedial treatment when it involves creative and therapeutic activities as well as a knowledge of the child's background, problems and parental attitudes. It is impossible to carry out this approach during two or three lessons a week. It must not be forgotten, however, that children, on occasion, do require good teaching in the skills of reading. Unfortunately, many teachers are able to provide opportunities for the child to learn to read but have little idea how to teach reading. Priority should be given to the provision of courses of study in the teaching of reading in Colleges of Education. Naturally, this is given to those who intend to teach in infant schools but, generally speaking, there is very little provision for those who intend to enter junior and secondary schools.

The solution, therefore, is in the hands of the class teacher. I would suggest that it is the teacher who has the greatest

[1] Collins, J. E., *The Effects of Remedial Education,* Oliver & Boyd, Edinburgh, 1961.

[2] Lovell, K., Johnson, E. & Platts, B., 'A summary of a study of the reading ages of children who had been given remedial teaching', *Brit. J. Educ. Psychol.,* **32**, 66–7, 1962.

[3] Lovell, K., Byrne, C. & Richardson, B., 'A further study of the educational progress of children who had received remedial education', *Brit. J. Educ. Psychol.,* **33**, 1, 3–9, 1963.

[4] Cashdan, V. & Pumfrey, P. D.; 'Some effects of the remedial teaching of reading', *Educ. Res.,* **11**, 2, 138–142, 1969.

influence on a child's progress in reading, and the most important criterion involved in the teaching of reading is not so much the method being adopted, but rather the individual teacher's faith and enthusiasm in the method she is using.

2

A selection of reading games and activities

All activities and experiences provided for the child should be such that they encourage the child to want to learn to read.

During the stage of reading preparation, the child should have experiences which will help to develop his powers of visual and auditory discrimination, his levels of spoken vocabulary, listening, and social and emotional maturity.

The child should be in a classroom environment which provides colourful books of all kinds, covering a wide range of interests. He should be encouraged to handle books, look at pictures and talk about what he sees. The teacher reads stories, talks about pictures and encourages the child to talk about them. The child should be surrounded by colourful and interesting displays and various objects carrying labels, phrases and sentences.

The making of books is a very important activity in learning to read. Such books are made from the child's own ideas, words and sentences. The teacher encourages the child to talk and write about as many of his interests and activities as possible so that he builds up a vocabulary of words which are meaningful and interesting.

Before or during the time children begin to read their first readers, it is suggested that they become accustomed to the words contained in such readers. Many first readers have much supplementary material which will help to provide the necessary extra experience and practice. Many games and activities can be based on this supplementary material and other teacher-made material.

The teacher should study the various games and activities available, analyse the skills which they promote and the level of difficulty which they represent.

A game or activity indulged in for too long a period without substitution of new items, can lead to the overlearning of something known very well already. If the game or activity is such that a child can add new items and thus use forms of adaptation the value of the material is further extended.

When a teacher is choosing or making the various games, activities and other aids to reading, he must keep in mind the individual requirements of each child. It is fully appreciated, of course, that a teacher with 30 or more children in the class will have to cater for the needs of the average children. It is hoped, however, that the many suggestions contained in this work will help the teacher to overcome some of these problems.

Although the following games and activities are discussed under separate headings, it is not intended that they should be thought of as completely independent activities. All such activities occur in all aspects of the curriculum. The following games and activities are merely suggestions so that the teacher may elaborate on them.

The following are points which the teacher should have in mind when deciding upon the various reading games and activities which he wishes to use:

1. Do they provide exercises for the development of preparation for reading?
2. Do they place the onus of active learning on the child?
3. Do they help to establish word recognition?
4. Do they help in diagnosing a child's difficulties?

5. Do they involve activities concerning listening, speaking and writing?
6. Is learning carefully graded?
7. Are the various skills being taught rather than being tested?
8. Do they provide opportunities for self-evaluation?
9. Are the instructions simple and clear enough for the child to involve himself in the activity?
10. Do they provide opportunities for silent as well as oral participation?

(See Appendix C for a selection of commercially-produced reading materials.)

A. Preparation for reading

(i) HELPING LANGUAGE DEVELOPMENT

In order that reading will become enjoyable and meaningful, the teacher should attempt to ensure that the words he wants the child to read are words found within the child's own vocabulary. The teacher should attempt to provide children with experiences that will lead to a rich and varied language development. It should be hoped that the language of the children will include many words and ideas that will be met in the printed form.

Teachers appreciate that children of infant age who come from backgrounds that are intellectually and culturally adequate acquire language efficiency informally and quite incidentally. However, children from a culturally deprived background and the intellectually slow are not so fortunate.[1, 2, 3] More and more educationists advocate the use of more procedures for stimulating the language development of children.

[1] Morris, J. M., *Standards and Progress in Reading,* N.F.E.R., London, 1966.
[2] Kellmer-Pringle, M. L. *et al., 11,000 Seven-year Olds,* Longmans, London, 1966.
[3] Goodacre, E. J., *Teaching Beginners to Read: Report No. 2, Teachers and their Pupils' Home Background,* N.F.E.R., London, 1967.

It will be advantageous to keep the following points in mind when providing activities to help language development:

1. The various games and activities are not intended to replace the regular daily activities but rather to supplement them.
2. The activities should provide opportunities for more talk than usual.
3. The games and activities should be pupil-centred.
4. Opportunities should be given for spontaneity in speech.
5. Children should have the opportunity of joining in games and activities involving repetition.

1. *Talking about pictures*

The teacher encourages the child to talk about a large, coloured picture. The children discuss the main theme of the picture and the various actions of the figures in the picture. The children are asked to give the colours used in the picture, and are asked questions relating to the weather, the season etc. A few children may be able to make up a short story of one, two or three sentences. The 'Chameleon Street Cellograph Picture Making Outfit', (Philip & Tacey Ltd.), is extremely useful for this kind of work.

2. *Instructions*

The teacher asks children to carry out simple instructions. For example, a child is told to walk to the back of the classroom, turn right, pick up the toy and put it on the teacher's desk. The remainder of the class watch carefully to see if an error is made. The instructions may be varied and gradually increased in difficulty. An attempt should be made to make the instructions as interesting and amusing as possible. This encourages accurate listening not only on the part of the child carrying out the instruction, but also by the other children in the class.

3. *Describing Words*

The teacher attempts to elicit from the children as many descriptive words as possible. A familiar object is shown to the children, (e.g. a balloon) and the teacher asks the following questions:

> 'Who can tell me what this is?'
> 'What colour is it?'
> 'What shape is it?'
> 'Is it heavy?' etc.

The children's answers will provide such words as 'balloon', 'yellow', 'round', 'light', 'thin' etc.

4. *Story Endings*

The teacher reads a short story to the children leaving it unfinished. The children are asked to give their own versions of the ending of the story. For example, 'Simon lived on a farm. One day, he was walking in a field. He was going to see . . .'

5. *Play Acting*

The children are asked to give simple lines for various parts in the dramatization of a familiar story. Various situations and happenings may be acted. For example, 'at the doctor's', 'at the dentist's', 'a policeman finding a lost child', 'a television programme', 'personal happenings' etc. Children should be given the opportunity of providing their own material and the classroom should be adapted to represent the various scenes.

6. *Using the Tape Recorder*

The teacher can encourage the children to describe things and events. The children should be encouraged to talk about their likes and dislikes, journeys they have made etc.

Using the tape recorder, ask the children to say,

'My name is . . . I live at . . . What is your name?'

The child passes the microphone to the next child and the procedure is repeated.

The tape recorder provides a means of bringing different speech models to the children. This can be done by giving the children opportunities for reading stories. This provides an opportunity for the children to listen, hear and understand various speech models. The tape recorder is also useful for helping young children to evaluate their own speech patterns.

The Tape Recorder in the Classroom[1] is a useful book which provides many further suggestions.

7. *Using Puppets*

Puppets may be used to draw attention to certain topics. They may be used to encourage the 'handlers' to talk. In this respect, puppets may be useful in helping to 'draw out' those children who are inclined to remain withdrawn and who may find it easier to express themselves through the use of puppets.

8. *What Would You Do?*

The teacher thinks up a situation and asks the children for whom they would send if, for example, their house was on fire; a water pipe burst; there was a gas leak etc.

9. *Classifications*

The teacher divides the class up into teams. Questions are asked as follows;

> 'What word can we use for all the things we wear?'
> 'What word can we use for "dog", "cat", "cow", "horse", "elephant" and "monkey"?'

One mark is given for each correct answer.

(ii) HELPING VISUAL DISCRIMINATION

The teacher is able to appreciate the child's ability in visual

[1] Weston, J., *The Tape Recorder in the Classroom*, National Committee for Audio-Visual Aids, London, 1968.

discrimination through the use of various games and activities. A knowledge of a child's skills in visual discrimination will enable the teacher to devise other games and activities which will help his progress in this field. A few reading schemes[1] have material to help the child in his skill to discriminate, but some children may require more than this material offers. Some of the following games and activities ought to be helpful.

1. *Kim's Game* (This may have many other names.)

The teacher places four or five familiar objects on the desk or table and the child is given a few seconds to look at them. The child turns away and the teacher covers the objects with a cloth. The child has to remember as many objects as possible. There are many variations of this game. For example, the teacher takes one object away or covers up one object with an empty box. The time allowed and the number of objects hidden from view may vary so that the game is made easier or more difficult.

2. *Matching Shapes*

The teacher cuts out various shapes of various sizes. For example, squares, rectangles, circles, triangles, stars. The children are given these and asked to group them according to shape.

3. *Jigsaws*

The teacher takes two identical pictures. One picture is cut up into pieces of various sizes. The children are told to put the pieces together to correspond with the other picture. Such jigsaws may vary in difficulty from three simple pieces to more complex ones, e.g. commercially-produced jigsaws.

[1] *The Ladybird Key Words Reading Scheme,* Wills & Hepworth, Loughborough.

4. *Look and Draw*

The teacher draws a large shape or symbol on the blackboard. For example, a circle in a square. This should be quite easy for the children to draw. They are allowed to look at the drawing for several seconds, then it is covered. The children have to reproduce the drawing as accurately as possible. The shape may vary in difficulty and the time allowed to look at it may also vary.

5. *Colouring, Drawing and Tracing*

The children complete drawings with the use of templates and then colour them. Tracing is another useful exercise. One activity which most children enjoy is the joining of dots to form a picture.

6. *What Can We See?*

The teacher encourages children to observe a large picture very closely. Many children are inclined to lack concentration when observing pictures and fail to appreciate that the pictures are 'telling' stories.

7. *Sorting*

Words and pictures are given to groups of children. They are asked to sort the pictures and words into groups according to such headings as 'the farm', 'the kitchen', 'food', 'clothes' etc.

8. *Dominoes*

Children are asked to match symbol against symbol, picture against picture, letter against letter and picture against word.

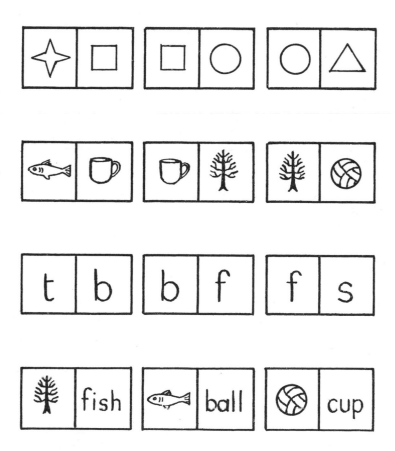

9. *Odd-Man-Out*

The teacher provides the children with cards containing a line of similar objects, symbols etc. The child is asked to find the 'odd-man-out'.

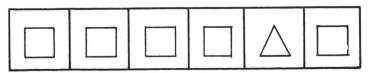

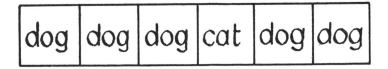

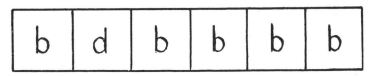

10. *Crossing Out*

The teacher provides the children with sheets of paper containing drawings of various animals. The teacher says,

'Cross out all the cats.'

Eventually, sheets of letters may be used. The teacher says,

'Cross out all the *f*'s.'

11. *What is Missing?*

The teacher provides the child with cards containing drawings of symbols, objects, letters, words etc. with missing pieces. The child has to indicate what is missing from one square on each card.

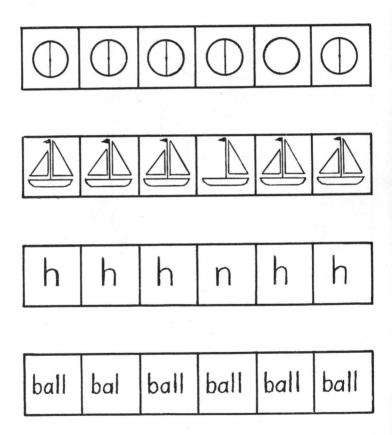

(iii) HELPING AUDITORY DISCRIMINATION

If the child is eventually going to tackle phonic work then he will require skill at auditory discrimination. If he is going to attempt to 'unlock' a word which he has not met before, it will be necessary for him to appreciate that a word has its own sound pattern, that this pattern may be broken down into a series of sounds which are arranged in a definite sequence, and that these sounds relate to the shapes of letters or a combination of such shapes.

The following are a few suggestions for helping the child to develop the skill of auditory discrimination.

1. *Misfits*

The teacher calls out a series of words beginning with the same initial sound, but the series contains one word which has a different initial sound. The children are asked to put up their hands if they have detected the 'misfit'. For example, 'tap', 'tin', 'toy', 'bat', 'top'. Another variation is the use of rhyming words. For example, 'get', 'let', 'met', 'cat', 'pet'.

2. *Sounds Around Us*

The children close their eyes and remain as quiet as possible. Ask the children to listen for and remember as many sounds as they can, inside and outside the classroom. When this activity is first used, the teacher may find that very few children have heard many sounds, but, eventually, they will be able to report on 'a passing lorry', 'people walking outside the school', 'whispering', 'sighing' etc. The tape recorder may be used for a whole series of exercises. The Remedial Supply Company[1] supply a tape – 'Pictures in Sound'.

3. *High and Low Sounds*

High and low notes produced on a piano can help the children in more specific discrimination. The teacher may produce

[1] The Remedial Supply Company, Dixon Street, Wolverhampton.

a sound at different pitches. There are many other ways of making different sounds which may be thought of by the teacher.

4. *Disguised Voices*

The teacher selects a child to recite a well-known nursery rhyme. The child is told to disguise his voice as much as he can. The remainder of the class sit with their eyes closed and attempt to discover the name of the child who is reciting.

5. *Recorded Sounds*

The teacher records many familiar sounds with the use of a tape recorder. For example, 'a door bell', 'animal noises', 'clock chimes', 'the school bell' etc. The children may either say what the sounds are or they may hold up a picture of the object etc.

6. *Choral Speaking*

The choral speaking of nursery rhymes and other poems may help children in auditory discrimination.

7. *Rhythms*

Percussion instruments may be used to help children to remember rhythms. The teacher may also tap out the rhythms and ask the children to repeat them. This may be followed by asking the children to march and dance to certain rhythms.

8. *'Listening' Walks*

During nature walks or other out-of-door-activities, children are asked to remember as many sounds as they can during periods of 'listening'. This exercise may be discussed back in the classroom.

(iv) HELPING LEFT/RIGHT ORIENTATION

Most children develop this skill without actual training, through incidental learning, through activities involved in play and bodily activities. However, some children come to school needing specific practice in this skill before making an attempt at reading. All activities involving hand-eye motor co-ordination will help. This may be done through games and playing with toys. Many other activities may be used such as tracing, folding along a line, cutting out shapes, cutting along a line etc.

The following are a few suggestions:

1. *Action Pictures*

The teacher should provide the child with series of action pictures which have to be followed from left to right. Comics, Annuals etc. contain such action pictures which are arranged from left to right. Other examples may be found in non-verbal intelligence tests. Eventually, the child may be given separate action pictures which he has to arrange in correct order from left to right in order to understand the sequence of the story. Certain individual pictures may help to encourage the left to right movement of the eye.

2. *Mazes*

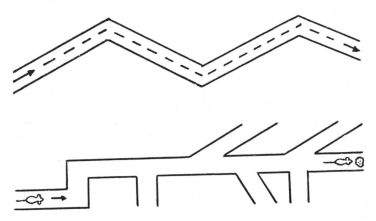

B. Word Recognition

Reading is based on the recognition of symbols. At first, the child may recognise the word or letter and later the phrase. In order to read with fluency and comprehension, a child must increase his level of ability in word recognition. A level should be reached with certain words so that the child's response becomes almost automatic. At the beginning stage of reading, the child should build up a sight vocabulary of words in common usage in his everyday speech. (See *Key Words to Literacy*[1].)

The Wordmaster Major[2] is a group learning aid for basic language skills and is a very useful reading aid designed for a wide range of class activities. This material supplements the various reading schemes already in use in the classroom.

The aid consists of 14 large cards with 20 words of varying colour and size printed on each card. The cards provide a good

[1] McNally, J. & Murray, W., *Key Words to Literacy*, Schoolmaster Publishing Co., Ltd., London, 1962.

[2] Wordmaster Major, Macdonald Educational, 49/50 Poland Street, London, W1A 2LG.

supply of words in common usage and found in the early stages of reading schemes, together with words used less frequently but which have interesting visual shapes.

Groups playing the Wordmaster game may vary in size from two to a group of ten or more. These groups may consist of children with very little reading ability or those who are quite fluent readers.

A child may use any of the following means of recognising words and frequently will adopt a combination of two or more.

1. The pattern of the word.
2. The length of the word.
3. The initial letter of the word.
4. The final letter of the word.
5. Letter groupings, e.g. 'oo' as in 'book'.
6. Contextual clues.

The following is a selection of games and activities designed to help to increase the child's ability in word recognition.

1. *The Weather Chart*

The teacher should prepare a cyclostyled chart for each member of the class. One chart per month would be suitable. The chart should be so planned that there is sufficient space for printing the days of the week and for printing in a word describing the day's weather. The children may also use illustrations to describe the weather, e.g. an umbrella, the sun, a cloud etc.

2. *A Picture Dictionary*

The teacher or child makes an indexed scrap-book. Pictures are cut from newspapers, magazines etc. The scrap-book contains words which the child is using. If the word is 'rabbit', the child pastes the picture of the rabbit on the 'R' page. At a later date, the teacher may give the child cards on which the words, which have been learned, are printed. Now the child has to find the picture and place the correct word underneath.

3. *A Picture Scrap-Book*

The child builds up his own scrap-book. Each picture should have a word, phrase or sentence written near it.

4. *Special Interest Books*

If children are interested in special kinds of stories, such as farming, animal, sport or adventure, they may be encouraged to print relevant words, essential to their interests, in a special interest book.

5. *My Word-Book*

When a child learns a word, he prints this in his indexed word-book. Whenever possible, the words may be illustrated using pictures or the child's own drawings.

6. *Fishing*

Words are printed on cardboard 'fish'. Paper fasteners are attached to the heads of the fish. These are then put into a large fishbowl or cardboard box. The child uses a piece of string with a magnet at the end to catch the fish. If he can read the word printed on the fish, he keeps it, otherwise it must be thrown back. At a later stage, phrases and sentences may be used in place of words.

7. *Matchboxes*

Paste a word on the outside of a matchbox and then place a picture illustrating the word inside the matchbox. The child opens the matchbox to find what the word is. After a while, the child will be able to read the word without opening the box.

8. *Lucky Dip*

A large box is filled with small objects. The words corresponding to the objects are printed on cards and are placed either at the bottom of the blackboard or on a table. Each child closes his eyes and picks up an object. He must then find the corresponding word. Objects or pictures may be used.

9. *Treasure Hunt*

The teacher writes the first clue on the blackboard, e.g. 'Look in Mary's desk.' The second clue, in Mary's desk, may be, 'Look under teacher's book.' The other clues may be hidden in various places in the classroom. Eventually, the treasure is found.

10. *The Use of Flash Cards*

The teacher uses a set of 16 cards. Each member of a group of four children has four cards. The teacher holds up a card and says,

'Who has "boy"?'

The children study their cards. If the word is recognised, one pupil will say,

'I have "boy".'

But if the word is not recognised immediately, the children will compare their cards with the teacher's. When the teacher uses this approach, it ensures that all the children are involved.

11. *Word Snap*

Children are provided with an equal number of flash cards. Each player puts down a card in turn. When two cards with the same word are showing, the first player to say the word aloud, wins. The teacher should provide four cards for each word.

12. The teacher writes ten words on the blackboard. These words are taken from a set of flash cards. The flash cards are shared out amongst two teams of children. Each word is repeated two, three or four times on these flash cards. The teacher calls out one of the words from the blackboard without

pointing at it. If a child believes that he has the card, then he reads it aloud and walks out to match it with the word on the blackboard. The child wins a point for his team.

13. *Which Word?*

The teacher draws actions of various kinds on several cards. Three words are printed alongside each drawing. The child has to point or mark the correct word.

14. *Instruction Cards*

The teacher uses flash cards with verbs printed on them. She flashes the card with 'stand' on it and the first child to stand wins the card. The children may be divided up into small groups and one child may take the place of the teacher. At a later stage, the following may be used:

'Walk to the door.'

'Touch your ear.' etc.

15. *Picture Cards*

The teacher cuts out cards approximately 6″ × 4″. Children cut out pictures of their own particular interests from newspapers, magazines, old books etc. Under each picture, a word or phrase describing the picture is printed by the teacher when the picture has been pasted on the card. The same word or phrase is printed on the reverse side of the card. The children are given the cards and learn to associate the word or phrase with the picture. At a later stage, the children are shown the reverse side displaying only the printed words.

16. *Find the Word*

The teacher places a number of small articles in a large envelope, e.g. key, chalk, pencil, button etc. The names of the articles are printed on the envelope. The child has to place each article by the correct word, and repeats those causing him difficulty until all are known. A number of envelopes may be used, graded in difficulty.

17. *Spinning Words*

Cut a piece of card into the shape of a regular octagon. Print

words along the edges and put a small stick through the centre. The children spin the card and read the word nearest to them when the card stops.

18. *Word Dice*

These are made of wood and different words are printed on each side. The children roll the dice and read the top word. These may be used in various forms of competition.

19. *The Clock-Face Game*

A cardboard clock-face is numbered 1 to 12 and fitted with one large hand. This may be held in place by using a metal fastener. Twelve words are printed alongside the clock-face, numbered from 1 to 12. The child spins the hand and waits to see near which number it stops. He then reads the corresponding word printed against this number.

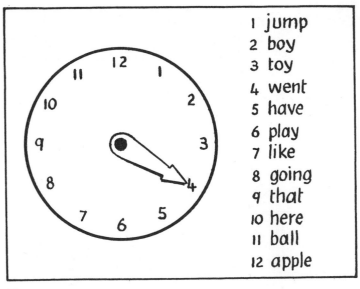

20. *The Football Game*

Draw a football pitch on a large card, $15'' \times 12''$, including goal posts. Across the pitch, parallel with the half-way line, mark about 8 straight lines approximately $1\frac{1}{2}''$ apart. Draw a football on a $1''$ square and place it at the centre of the pitch. Prepare small cards with a picture on one side and the word on the other and put them on the desk with the words uppermost. Each child takes a card and reads the word aloud, checking with the picture on the reverse side. If he is correct, he moves the football one space forward. The ultimate aim is to get the football into the goal. This game may be played either with two boys as opponents or one team against the other, or for a knock-out competition around the class.

21. *Adapted Games*

Ludo, snakes and ladders and other popular games may be adapted to form reading games. Give each child a sheet of paper with numbered words or sentences on it. Whatever number the child throws, he must read the word or sentence set against the corresponding number on the sheet of paper before he moves. Two dice may be used in order to provide more words or sentences.

22. *The Race Track*

Draw an oval race track with four lanes. Draw straight lines about $2''$ apart across the track and all the way around it. The four players are represented by four coloured, toy cars. Each boy moves his car one space forward if he reads a word correctly. Cards may be used with pictures on the reverse side.

23. *Making Sense*

Each child, in a group of three or more, is given a card with a single word on it which he can read. These cards have been selected by the teacher to make a sentence when put in the correct order. The children stand in front of the class holding up their cards and reading the words aloud. The remainder of the class will tell the card-holders to move to certain positions. The card-holders are then asked to read their cards once more – the result being a complete sentence.

24. *Individual Snap*

A pack of cards, each $4'' \times 2\frac{1}{2}''$, is made as follows:

One card has a drawing of a 'duck'. The word 'duck' is printed at the top right hand corner of the card with the initial letter 'd' cut out. A corresponding card without a drawing will have 'd' printed at the top left hand corner. When the card with the drawing of the duck is placed on top of the other

card, the word 'duck' is formed. (A self-correcting method may be adopted if one card is placed correctly on top of the other and a 'v' shape is cut out. This 'v' shape may be cut out at various other places when other cards are made.)

25. *Help-Yourself-Activities*

The teacher prepares activity cards containing problems, situations etc. for various activities. The activity cards are placed in a receptacle such as a cardboard box. The child is allowed to choose one card and carries out the activity. The teacher checks the child by observing his final accomplishment. The teacher should ensure that there is a continual supply of new cards with new ideas.

26. *Word Pairs.*

The teacher cuts pictures from newspapers, magazines, old books etc. and prints pairs of words on them. Words such as 'up, down', 'over, under', 'in, out', 'small, big' etc.

27. *Sorting*

Various words are printed on small cards and the children have to sort them under separate headings such as 'things we wear', 'things we eat' etc.

28. *A Key Words Display*

The most used words in everyday conversation and books should be learned as soon as possible. Many of these words appear very frequently in children's books but are not so easily committed to memory. The McNally and Murray list[1] is very useful.

Fasten a length of plastic curtain rail across the top of a wall-

[1] McNally, J. & Murray, W., *Key Words to Literacy*. Schoolmaster Publishing Co., Ltd., London, 1962.

about	back	call	day	fast	gave
after	bad	came	did	father	get
again	be	can	do	fell	girl
always	because	come	dog	first	give
all	been	could	don't	find	go
am	before		down	five	going
an	best			fly	good
and	big			for	got
another	bird			four	green
any	black			found	
are	blue			from	
as	boy				
ask	bring				
at	but				
away					

blackboard or on another convenient place in front of the classroom. The list of words may be hung from the curtain rail by means of plastic clothes pegs. These pegs may be attached to the rail by means of split curtain rings. When the lists are required, they may all be displayed to the class. When they are not required, they may be pulled across to one side.

29. *Making Sentences*

This is a useful activity for those children who are beginning

to read phrases and sentences. Two large envelopes contain two separate sets of cards. One set consists of phrase cards containing those words being used in the early stages of learning to read. The second set consists of pictures and words. The children make sentences from the phrase cards and picture cards. The pictures may be obtained from magazines etc.

30. *The Typewriter*

The typewriter can be a very useful reading aid if one is able to acquire an old one still in working order. (Ask the children. It is surprising what some parents are prepared to give to the school when the article has outlived its usefulness in the home.)

There are some children who try hard to read without great success yet they enjoy typing captions for the nature table, class newspapers or displays etc. This helps to make reading more meaningful for them.

C. Phonics

There are certain abilities which children should have in order that they will understand and be able to apply the phonic method of reading. They should be able to appreciate rhyme, discriminate between letter sounds, blend sounds and associate a sound with its visual representation.

Because a child is limited in the number of words he can commit to memory, some skill in phonic analysis and synthesis is essential[1]. The child must, eventually, be able to analyse a word into its sounds and then be able to blend sounds to make whole words. At all stages of reading, a child will encounter words which are unfamiliar; therefore exercises and practice in the fundamentals of phonic work are essential.

Even young children of infant school age have a limited capacity for combining sounds, but they need an abundance of

[1] Chall, J., *Learning to Read*. McGraw-Hill, New York, 1967.

46

experience and practice before they can use a 'word attack' consisting of phonic analysis and synthesis. As a child gradually increases his sight vocabulary, he can be helped to notice similarities and differences in the pattern and sound of words. A few of the following suggestions are probably better carried out as the occasion arises and not as daily dosages of drill.

31. *Group Rhyming*

The teacher begins by saying aloud a certain word, e.g. 'fight'. The children have to think of words rhyming with this word. This continues until all the possibilities have been exhausted.

32. *Word Puzzles*

The teacher reads out several clues and the children have to guess what the object is. For example,

'I have four legs, two arms and I am sat on. What am I?'

Initial Sounds

33. Ask the children to tell you with what sound certain words begin. The teacher pronounces such words as 'bed', 'bus', 'big' etc. The teacher then asks the children to give other words which begin with the same sound. The teacher may also ask the children to feel the position of their lips and tongue when saying a word.

34. The teacher places flash cards at the bottom of the blackboard or in a position where they may be seen by the class. She pronounces a word and asks a child to pick up a card containing a word which begins with the same sound as the one pronounced.

35. The teacher writes several consonants on the blackboard, e.g. 'f', 't', 's', 'b' etc. She says a word and a child is asked to point at the letter on the blackboard which gives the 'beginning' sound of the word.

36. In a list of six words, five begin with the same initial sound. The children have to find the 'stranger'. For example, 'kettle', 'kite', 'kangaroo', 'lorry', 'kipper'. The same activity may be used with rhyming words.

37. The teacher and the children play a game of 'sound snap'. The teacher gives the sound and the children search for the card with the correct letter on it.

38. The teacher draws various pictures and then cyclostyles them. If possible three or four sheets of pictures should be available. The initial sounds (letters) for all the pictures on one sheet are printed at the bottom. The child has to select the letter which gives the initial sound of the picture. He prints this under each picture.

The teacher may vary this activity by printing the appropriate words underneath the pictures, but with the initial letter missing. The child has to find the missing letter and print it in the correct place in order to complete the word.

39. Place five or six objects on a tray and hold the tray up so that the children may see all the objects. The names of the objects may start with whatever sounds have just been studied, e.g. '*b*all', '*c*up', '*d*oll'. Ask the children to close their eyes and then take one object from the tray. The children must find what object is missing. They must not give its name, but its initial sound only. Then they must describe its appearance.

40. Draw a picture on the blackboard and ask the child to copy the drawing on the paper in front of him. Ask the child to label each object with the letter that represents the initial sound of the object's name. Encourage the children to add more objects to the drawing and to label them. This activity may be used to concentrate on one initial sound rather than many.

41. Print two letters on the blackboard or on a card. Leave a space between the letters, e.g. Λ   T. The children are asked to write as many words as they can that begin and end with these letters. For example, 'ant', 'art', 'aunt', 'about'. If a competition is involved, one point may be given for each letter added.

42. *Word Families*
Several word families and three or four consonants are put in envelopes. The envelopes are given to a group of six children. The first child to assemble all his words wins.

D

The class may be divided up into small groups. Some groups will have envelopes containing consonants, and others envelopes containing word families. The groups with the consonants move amongst those with word families until they meet partners who are able to combine their cards with the consonants and thus make words.

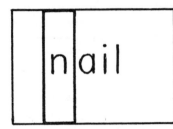

43. *Initial Blends*

The teacher pronounces words with the same initial blends, e.g. '*sh*op', '*sh*eep', '*sh*ed', '*sh*ip'. The teacher asks the children with what sound all these words begin. She then asks them to give other words with the same initial blends. When two-letter blends are known, the teacher may move on to three-letter blends, e.g. '*str*ing', '*str*aw', '*str*eet'.

44. *Final Sounds*

Cut out cards, 6″ × 6″. On these cards, paste pictures cut out from old magazines, books etc. Underneath each picture, print its name with the final letter missing. At the bottom of the card, print all the missing final letters. The child has to select the correct final letter for each word. Another approach is for the teacher to prepare similar work and cyclo-style several copies of each card. In this case, the child may write in the missing letters.

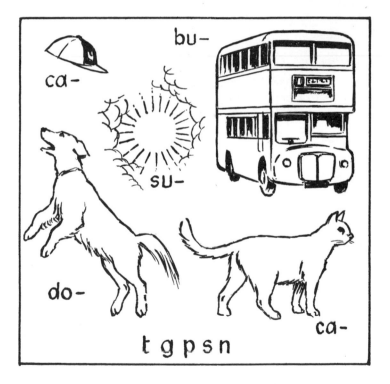

45. Children may be helped to learn final sounds through rhymes. The teacher says the word 'day' and asks the children to say words which end with the same sound. The teacher may write these words on the blackboard so that the children may appreciate the combination of letters which gives the same sound, e.g. 'day', 'gay', 'hay', 'may', 'say'.

A further variation is for the teacher to print words on small cards. Four teams are given an equal number of cards. The first player reads from his cards. If another player has a word which rhymes, then he must give the card to the first player. The winning player is the one with most cards at the end of the game.

46. The teacher writes several words on the blackboard, e.g. 'ring', 'sing', 'cold', 'wing', 'sold' etc. The teacher asks the children to come out and join those words ending with the same sound. (This activity may be used with initial sounds.)

47. The teacher cuts out pieces of card approximately 5″ × 4″. Three or more words are printed on each card. The child is able to see that identical sounds may be found in many different words.

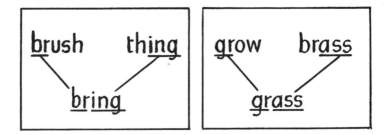

48. *Sound Lotto*

Cut out six pieces of card, $6\frac{1}{2}'' \times 6\frac{1}{2}''$, (or as many cards as required). Cut out 'Key Pictures', $2'' \times 3''$, from a magazine, old books etc. and paste a Key Picture at the top of each card. Divide the remainder of the card into six blank spaces, $2'' \times 2''$. Then cut out other pictures each showing an object whose name begins with one of the initial sounds of the Key Pictures. Paste these on pieces of card, $2'' \times 2''$. Give one Key Picture to each child. The other smaller cards are shuffled and placed face down on the desk or table. A 'caller' picks up the first card and names the object portrayed. Each child must listen carefully, identify the initial sound, and whenever his Key Picture begins with the same sound, he claims the card. The winner is the first child to cover his six blank spaces.

49. *Anagrams*

Sheets or cards are prepared containing drawings or pictures from magazines, catalogues etc. of common objects. Opposite each drawing or picture the appropriate word is printed, but the letters are scrambled. The children have to unscramble the letters and make the correct words.

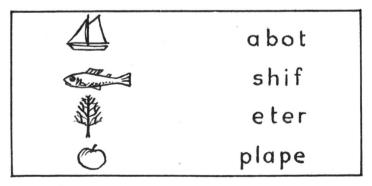

50. *Word Building Cards*

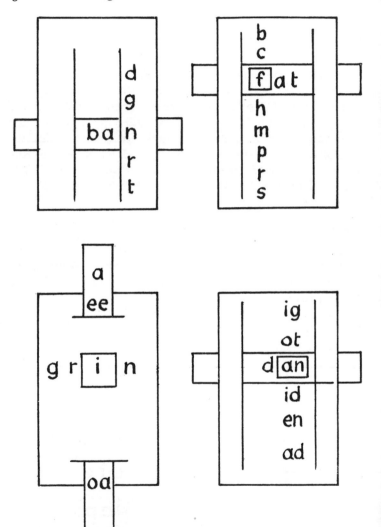

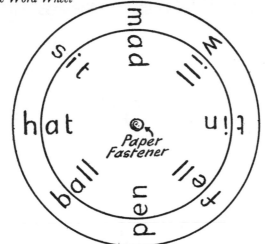

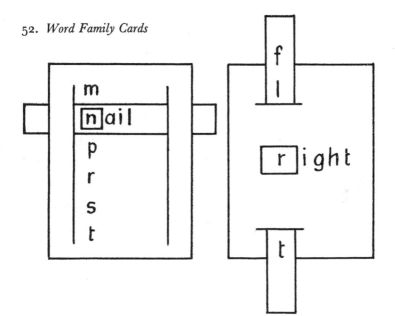

53. *Phonic Work Cards*

The teacher cuts out a piece of white cardboard, $8'' \times 8''$. The purpose of this card is to help children who are going to write about a certain topic. The most important words are listed on the right hand side and further words are listed in two further columns. The child will be able to appreciate the relationship between the word which he wishes to use and the other words containing the same sound.

My School		
tea	teach	teacher
ass	class	classroom
lay	play	playground
in	din	dinner
in	win	window
read	reading	reading-book
in	ink	sink
draw	drawing	drawing-book
air	hair	chair

54. *Rotating Letter Cubes*

Cut out ½″ wooden cubes from balsa wood or other material. Drill holes through the centres of these cubes. Print letters on each side of each cube. The teacher should give some thought to the letters he wishes to print on the cubes. The aim is to provide sets of three or four cubes so that words may be built up either letter by letter or by adding different initial letters or final letters to a sound already contained in the first word made. Thread the sets of cubes on pieces of plastic curtain rail or pieces of elastic. The cubes may be turned around and many different words will be made.

55. *Word Sums*

The teacher writes the first eight or nine letters of the alphabet on the blackboard and gives each letter a number as follows:

a	b	c	d	e	f	g	h	i
1	2	3	4	5	6	7	8	9

Words are written on the blackboard using the numbers. The children have to decode and read the words.

For example:

2	9	7
b	i	g

2	1	7
b	a	g

6	5	5	4
f	e	e	d

3

The use of programmed materials and teaching machines

There is a growing volume of literature devoted to programmed learning and the use of teaching machines.[1, 2, 3, 4, 5]

A. Programmed Learning

Programmed learning is an attempt to make learning as easy as possible. The material is broken down into a series of short steps. Each step is so small that the next step is not difficult and frequently the answer is to be found in the previous step.

The exponents of programmed learning put forward the following claims:

1. The programmed material demands constant activity on the part of the child because of a constant interchange between it and the child.

2. Programmed material insists that a step must be understood before the child can move on to the next step.

[1] Kay, H., Dodd, B. & Sime, M., *Teaching Machines and Programmed Instruction*. Penguin Books Ltd., Harmondsworth, 1968.

[2] Romiszowski, A. J., *The Selection and Use of Teaching Aids*. Kogan Page, 1968.

[3] Leedham, J. & Unwin, D., *Programmed Learning in the Schools*. Longmans, 1967.

[4] Roucek, J. S., (Ed.), *Programmed Teaching*. (*A Symposium on Automation in Education*.) Peter Owen, London, 1966.

[5] Goldsmith, M., (Ed.), *Mechanisation in the Classroom*. (*An Introduction to Teaching Machines and Programmed Learning*.) Souvenir Press, London, 1963.

3. A child is continually motivated because he is informed immediately of the success or failure of his response.

4. A child can use programmed material at his own pace.

5. Programmed material creates a situation as similar as possible to the idea of one teacher to one pupil. If a child is unable to have a teacher to himself, he can have a programme which will tell him whether he is correct or otherwise.

6. Programmed material has 'feed-back', that is, if the programme is incorrect or too difficult for the child, this is quickly made apparent. There is not the same time-lag as a child would experience in the normal classroom situation where he has to wait for the teacher to attend to him.

7. Programmed material gives the teacher opportunities to spend more time with children who require his individual attention.

Programmed reading materials can be found in three forms – material used in a teaching machine, material on separate cards, and material in the form of a workbook or book.

Some programmes begin with a phonic approach, others offer routine practice and require the guidance of the teacher. The teacher must consider whether the material is suitable for (a) children who move on quickly and thus are able to leave out sections of the material and, (b) slower children who require to make small steps in order that the ideas are firmly understood. The teacher must also consider whether the content of the material holds the child's interest, whether a child is notified of his mistakes and is able to correct himself and, whether the written work involved in the material is suitable for the child and reinforces his learning. What is most important is that the teacher appreciates what the material demands from the child, what it contributes to the acquisition of skills and its level of motivation.

The Construction of Simple Programmed Reading Material

Simple programmed reading material may be made using the word-cue/picture-prompt idea. Divide the pages of an exercise book into two halves. Turn to the first page and at the top right hand corner print a simple word, e.g. 'bat'. On the reverse side paste a picture of a bat or use a simple line drawing. The picture gives immediate reinforcement to the response. The child works along the top of the book to the back, turns the book over, and works to the front. Confirmation of each response is in the form of a picture on the reverse side of each page.

The Programmed Reading Kit[1]

In recent years, there has been a growth in programmed reading material with a basically phonic approach.[2, 3, 4, 5]

In Stott's words, *The Programmed Reading Kit* is an attempt 'to work out a fresh approach to the teaching of reading which breaks away from the classic stereotypes of alternative methods'.[6] The Kit is a set of materials designed to impart phonic knowledge and to encourage the growth of phonic skills. Yet the approach does not use reading books. The material is arranged into individual and group games which are largely self-corrective.

Stott and others have based *The Programmed Reading Kit* on an investigation with a small group of boys from a school for the educationally subnormal, who had made little or no

[1] *The Programmed Reading Kit* by D. H. Stott, Holmes-McDougall, Edinburgh, 1962.

[2] *The Clifton Audio/Visual Reading Programme* by R. I. Brown & G. E. Bookbinder, ESA, Pinnacles, Harlow, Essex 1968.

[3] 'Dialogue 1', *An Aural-Oral Course in Phonics* by A. Brogan & E. Hatchkiss, Chester Electronic Laboratories Inc., Chester, Conn, 1963.

[4] *Lift Off to Reading* by W. Woolman, S.R.A. Inc., Chicago, 1966.

[5] *Programmed Reading* by C. D. Buchanan, Sullivan Associates – obtainable from McGraw-Hill, London, 1963–66.

[6] *Roads to Literacy* by Stott, D. H., Holmes-McDougall, Edinburgh, 1964.

progress in learning to read. Stott felt that if he could discover the points at which difficulties arose, and the means by which these difficulties might be overcome, he might possibly discover the fundamental processes involved in learning to read. It was thought that as a result of observing these boys, the processes involved in reading could be detected whereas, with normal children, these processes take place so rapidly that it is more difficult to detect them.

Because it was found that these boys exhibited slowness at every step, the learning process had to be broken down into its simplest elements.

Therefore, apparatus was devised which provided step by step stages so that the boys could appreciate what had to be learned and practise it in order to consolidate the learning. These boys had experienced a long history of failure. The apparatus had to be such that from the beginning success was possible as a result of a small effort.

The Kit consists of a series of 30 teaching aids and is the result of 10 years' research into the sticking points and difficulties which children meet in learning to read. The complete Kit of 30 pieces of apparatus is sufficient for a group of 4 or 6 children, or more if they are at different stages or progress at different rates. All items may be ordered separately.

It is claimed that the Kit takes the child from a state of not even knowing what is meant by sounds to a reading level of about 9 years.[1]

Children use the material for playing games. Learning is self-corrective so that a child teaches himself or a group will teach each other. As a child masters each item, he colours in a corresponding section on his Progress Card. I found that it is more motivating to award a 'star' which the child sticks on his card.

The learning processes involved in this Kit are finely pro-

[1] Stott, D. H., *Manual for the Programmed Reading Kit.* Holmes-McDougall, Edinburgh, 1962.

grammed so that the child may move on quite easily from one stage to the next. The Kit's self-learning features have a very important attribute in that a class at very different stages may be kept productively occupied without needing constant attention. The letter-sound associations are mastered naturally, and are acquired in an almost unconscious manner. Stott suggests that a child should not be taught the sounds of individual letters, but allowed to learn them incidentally as a result of associating the names of objects with their illustrations. However, I have found it more beneficial occasionally to tell the child that a letter has a specific sound. The key to the method involved in the Kit, therefore, is the building of phonic-sight habits.

I have found the Kit very useful because it may be used as supplementary material for any other approach or with any particular reading scheme. The most useful part of the Kit for a teacher who is confronted with the 'beginning reading' stage is contained in the first 14 items, i.e. sets 1 and 2. The games contained in these two sets provide the amount of repetition needed for thorough learning.

I have found certain items to be exceptionally useful. These are Touch Cards, Morris Cards, Port-Holes and the Brick Wall Game.

The Touch Cards are used to teach letters and sounds and to give children opportunities for playing games which will teach them the association between letter and sound. The Morris Cards provide a follow-up game after the Touch Cards have been used. These cards are to help the child to appreciate that a particular letter may be the initial sound for many words. The Port-Holes help the child to establish the phonic sight habits of two-letter word parts. The Brick Wall Game helps the child to blend letters and form words and, later, to use consonant digraphs and blends.

Touch Cards

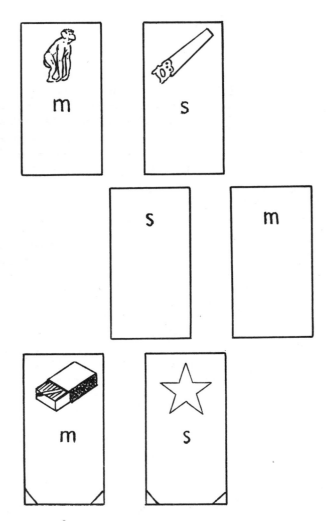

Morris Cards

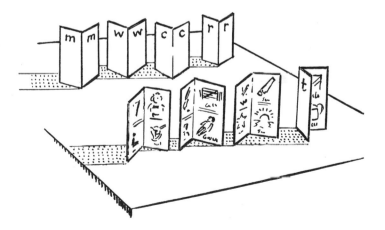

Port-Holes

Having used the Kit for several years, I would suggest that it may be very useful for children who have experienced a long history of failure in reading with the more traditional approaches. Although most children learn to read by various methods and, of course, in some cases, no method at all, a surer foundation may be laid by this programmed reading kit.

B. Teaching Machines

It is frequently suggested that the purest form of communication in education is seen in the one-to-one tutoring relationship. In such a situation, the teacher can respond, correct, guide, encourage and adapt to such a degree that the level of inter-communication becomes very high indeed. How often, however, is the teacher in a position to give as much individual attention as he wishes? Attempts are being made to overcome this problem through the introduction of mechanical devices.

More and more mechanical devices are being used as aids to the teaching of reading. Teachers are supplementing printed materials with such aids as records, tapes, films, filmstrips, overhead projectors, television etc. There has been an increasing manufacture and use of teaching machines.

The main advantages of teaching machines designed for individual use are:

(a) the child may work independently.
(b) he can proceed at his own rate.
(c) his responses to questions are checked immediately.
(d) errors are corrected at once.

Many teaching machines are designed for use with programmed materials[1]. A few are simple boxes containing rolls of questions and answers and these are usually rolled from the top to the bottom of the box, one question at a time, using a single knob. A second turn of the knob reveals the correct response and then the next question. Other machines use sets of cards.

One of the frequent criticisms of teaching machines is that they will reduce the teacher to a glorified attendant of the machine. The stimulation and excitement of helping a child grasp a concept will be modified until the teacher feels that she is nothing more than a switch operator. There is little doubt that the role of the teacher will be different when teaching machines are used, but the teacher should have more efficient means of determining learning handicaps and more resources available to help her. Teachers have depended for years on workbooks, visual aids and flash cards as important adjuncts to their

[1] *The New Craig Reader*, Craig Research Inc., California. Distributed by International Tutor Machines Ltd., Ashford, Middlesex.

programmes and eventually teaching machine programmes should provide firm bases from which to work.

Effective teaching machines are designed to aid the child in finding the correct answer. Part of this assistance comes through orderly programming. The other part comes from hints, prompting and suggestions the machine can give. Since some children have not developed skilful use of their auditory and visual senses, they must deal with the conceptual world largely in terms of concrete stimuli. The teaching machine can provide much of the concreteness necessary for comprehension until other fundamentals are mastered. In this sense, the machine can be effective in aiding the child and helping him to overcome the difficulties of his verbal, visual and auditory deficiences.

(See Appendix A for a selection of teaching machines.)

(i) THE CANTERBURY MK. II TEACHING MACHINE[1]

The Canterbury Teaching Machine (Fig. 1) employs a simple rugged mechanism, needs no maintenance or electricity and is easily used by very young children. The machine has a large frame area and it is very suitable for diagrams and pictures. A Word Recognition Programme is available, but the machine is designed for teachers to write their own programmes. A 50 frame programme can be written for about 25p: Each frame is on a separate card and it is quite simple to write a programme for the machine[2].

Even though a particular programme may require variation and alteration after a trial run, these may be effected by either writing extra cards or rewriting existing ones. The use of separate cards avoids the necessity of rewriting a whole programme. The machine's greatest virtue is its flexibility. A programme may be amended to suit different groups of children.

[1] The Canterbury Mk. II Teaching Machine. ESA, Pinnacles, Harlow, Essex.

[2] *Writing a Programme for the Canterbury Mk II Teaching Machine* (Free Booklet), ESA, Pinnacles, Harlow, Essex.

The simplest form of programme one may produce is a Drill Programme for word recognition. A question is asked and the child selects one out of a maximum of four answers. (See example below.)

this is a

A. ham
B. hat
C. hut
D. hoop

If the child has the correct answer, the card falls out of sight and the next card is exposed, otherwise it remains until the child selects the correct answer. Word recognition cards may be used in any order and they may be shuffled to provide variation. (Actually, this is not programmed learning because the steps do not follow on from each other, but the machine is very useful in so far as it provides an efficient way of learning.)

Linear programmes may be made for this machine. A linear programme is a step by step system. Each frame follows on from the previous one. Certain information is presented and a question is required to be answered. Once more the child has a choice of four answers and only the correct response will allow the card to fall. It is not always necessary to give a choice of four answers, a 'yes' or 'no' answer may be given.

It is claimed by the manufacturer that nothing can go wrong with the machine. From a mechanical point of view, this is correct, but the cards are so fragile that they may be easily damaged and I had to spend some time loading the machine myself.

(ii) THE ESATUTOR TEACHING MACHINE[1]

The Esatutor (Fig. 2) is a linear teaching machine and programmes may be used involving a carefully prepared step by step system. At each step, a problem is set and a clue is given so that the child has a very high chance of making the correct response. When the machine is operated by a simple hand-operated mechanism, the pupil's answer moves under a perspex window where it may be checked, but not altered, by comparing it with the correct answer which appears in the answer window. The child ticks his answer if his response is correct. At the same time, a new question appears and the child repeats the process.

Specially printed programmes are available, but it is wise for the teacher to produce his own. Blank programme cards are available in packs of 50. These are of thick card and will withstand much use. Printed packs of answer paper may be obtained, but the machine will also take ordinary paper cut to $8\frac{1}{4}'' \times 3''$. Each sheet of paper will take six answers on each side.

Reading programmes may be so designed that each step depends upon the child's having assimilated the steps already taken.

A set of cards is placed in the machine and the child is able to see the first question and the picture-aid. He answers the question on the answer paper in the machine and then moves the card forward by moving the control knob. His answer moves under the perspex window where it may be checked with the correct answer which has appeared in the answer

[1] The Esatutor Teaching Machine. ESA, Pinnacles, Harlow, Essex.

window. It is essential that young children should write their answers so that they may be compared with the correct ones when they appear in the answer window and so that the teacher may check the work later.

When one is preparing material for the machine it is important that the following general principles of programmed learning are kept in mind:

1. Ensure that the material is presented step by step in a carefully arranged order.

2. Ensure that at each step the child is given sufficient information to enable him to make an active response before moving on to the next step.

3. Ensure that the learner knows immediately whether his response is correct or otherwise.

The Esatutor may provide a form of individual attention for children and it enables the teacher to spend more of her time giving individual attention to a few more children in her class. This machine ensures that the bright child may move on quickly, while the slower reader may work at his own speed.

(iii) THE LANGUAGE MASTER[1, 2]

The Language Master (Fig. 3) is an audio-visual teaching aid consisting of a dual track magnetic recorder and a playback unit. It uses a card with a dual track magnetic stripe along the base, text and illustrations.

The stripe contains the spoken word corresponding with whatever is printed on the card. This card may be simply 'fed' into the Language Master and it passes through the machine automatically. The recorded voice repeats the word for the pupil. This may be repeated again and again if required. The pupil may repeat the words, record them and play them back

[1] The Language Master. Bell & Howell, Alperton House, Bridgewater Road, Wembley, Middlesex.

[2] There is now a new version of the machine. This is the Language Master Model 701, made in Japan and distributed by Bell & Howell.

so that he may immediately compare his own pronunciation with the correct one.

The Language Master has three main assets:

1. It may be used quite easily by very young children.

2. It may easily be moved from one position to another and from one classroom to another.

3. An important asset is its flexibility. The teacher may easily prepare his own programmes.

The *Ladybird Key Words Reading Scheme* has been programmed for use with the Language Master. Key Words are available on Language Master taped cards with attractive illustrations.

Fifty blank cards or a prepared reading scheme, (the *Leedham Reading Scheme*), may be obtained. This reading scheme consists of 66 cards and 6 booklets.

The *Leedham Reading Scheme* may be used individually, or in small groups of two or three. The children are encouraged to work quite freely through the cards and matching booklets. The length of a lesson with the Language Master depends upon the child's ability and can vary from 10 to 15 minutes.

Even though the *Leedham Reading Scheme* is well-prepared and useful, I would suggest that a teacher should prepare his own reading programme from a supply of blank cards. A reading programme may be so planned that children are helped with their basic abilities in reading and spelling. The children may become involved in seeing, hearing, speaking and writing words and fully understanding their meanings. When such a reading programme is planned, it is useful to keep the following points in mind:

1. The children should be able to look and listen with comprehension. During the early stages of learning, they look at a picture and a word whilst listening to a recorded voice telling them what it is.

2. The children should be able to vocalise and record with

Fig. 1. The Canterbury Mk. II Teaching Machine

Fig. 2. The Esatutor Teaching Machine

*Fig. 3.
The Language
Master*

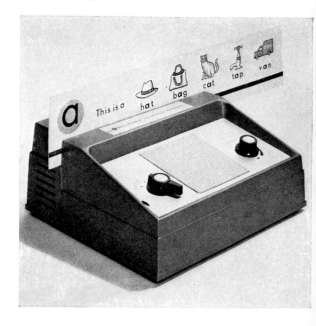

Fig. 4. The Stillitron

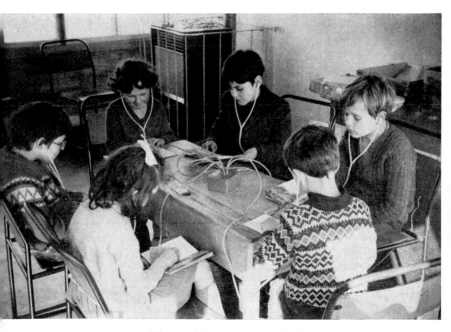

Fig. 5. The Primary Audio Set

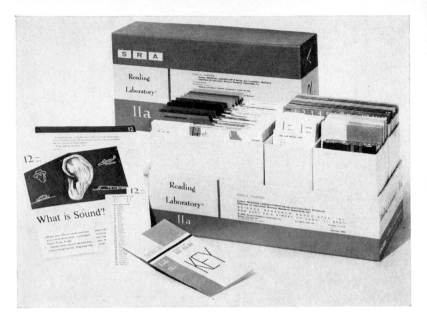

Fig. 6. SRA Reading Laboratory IIa

Fig. 7. SRA Reading Laboratories in use

comprehension. They record each word using the picture as an aid and later record without the aid of a picture.

3. The children should be given the opportunity of using learned words in carefully graded sentences.

The 'look and say' method of teaching reading demands that words and phrases be presented in a graduated order, at a pace adapted to the individual child, in a manner that permits feedback of results (preferably immediately). Conventional classroom teaching cannot ordinarily meet all these conditions, but the Language Master can.

Unfortunately, the use of the Language Master can interfere with other children in the class and it should be equipped with an adaptor which could be used for headphones. It is a very useful aid, but considering its cost, I would suggest that a teacher would probably have more value for money if he were prepared to experiment with a tape recorder and headphones.

(iv) THE STILLITRON[1]

The Stillitron (Fig. 4), which is used with Stillit responding books, is approximately ten inches long by five inches wide. It consists of a printed-circuit plate and a head which contains two bulbs, two torch batteries and a stylus. The plate is placed under the page which is to be read. The pupil reads the text, and as he moves along, chooses with the stylus the answers to a series of questions. If he is correct, a green light shines and, if he is wrong, a red light shines. The pupil knows immediately whether he is correct or not. The pages are not marked in any way and the Stillitron is guaranteed to last a lifetime. It is claimed that the Stillitron's main virtue is in increasing motivation and reinforcement through immediate knowledge of the results.

Spirit Masters may be purchased. These enable the teacher to produce his own materials with the use of a spirit duplicator.

[1] Stillitron. Stillit Books Ltd., 72 New Bond Street, London, W.1.

The Mastergrid shows the teacher where to put 'responses' when he produces his own material.

The *Programmed Remedial Reading Texts*[1] are published in four parts. In the first two parts, single words are dealt with in ways that focus attention on individual letters. It is claimed that when the child uses the Stillitron to choose the correct letter in its correct position, the pupil's efforts are raised from the level of random guesswork to careful discrimination. By the end of Part 1, the child is beginning to use as a criterion the sound of a word. In Part 2, with the introduction of a colour-key system used throughout the rest of the texts, the child learns to associate a vowel sound, (e.g. in 'gun') first with a picture, (a grey gun), then the colour grey with pictures of objects containing that vowel sound, until, at the third learning step, he associates the colour grey with words that contain that vowel sound, (e.g. 'bus'). At the end of the sequence, the colour key is coding a sound, and may be used by the teacher in a wide variety of exercises. The seven vowels, whose variant spellings give the most trouble, are coded in this way. (See examples below.)

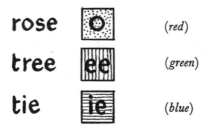

rose   *(red)*

tree   *(green)*

tie   *(blue)*

In Parts 3 and 4, the colour-key system leads the pupil from regular to irregular spellings and also gives practice in other sounds that do not need to make use of colour keys. They also

[1] Bhattacharya, S., *Programmed Remedial Reading Texts,* Stillit Books, London, 1967.

contain story material with a vocabulary based on *Key Words to Literacy*[1].

It is claimed that by the end of the texts, the pupil will have acquired mastery of 200 words where other methods may have failed, and will also have learned spelling principles rather than the memorising of individual words.

As a result of using the Stillitron and the *Programmed Remedial Reading Texts* with many children aged from seven to nine years of age, I have reached the following conclusions:

1. Several children, especially the youngest and those who lacked ability in manipulation, found it very difficult to fit the pages of the books into the Stillitron according to the guide lines on each page. When this is done incorrectly, the child does not receive a response because the marks where the stylus has to be placed are not synchronised with the printed circuit. I found, therefore, that I had to 'set up' each page for many children in my remedial groups.

2. Several of the drawings are not particularly obvious to the child. For example, in Book 1, the pictorial representation of 'log' and 'ink'. In the case of 'tail', I found that many non-readers believed that the word was 'monkey', even though there was a further clue in the picture. On page 5 a few pupils thought that the word 'ear' was 'head' because the drawing of an ear was lost in the picture of a girl's head even though the 'ear' was drawn in the shape of an 'e'.

3. In Book 2, I found that many pupils encountered other difficulties because of their regional pronunciations and I am quite sure that this problem will be accentuated in many other parts of the British Isles. For example:

'Find the picture with the same sound as str*aw*.' A few of the correct responses are 'door', 'four', 'sword'.

---

[1] McNally, J. & Murray, W., *Key Words to Literacy,* Schoolmaster Publishing Co. Ltd., London, 1962.

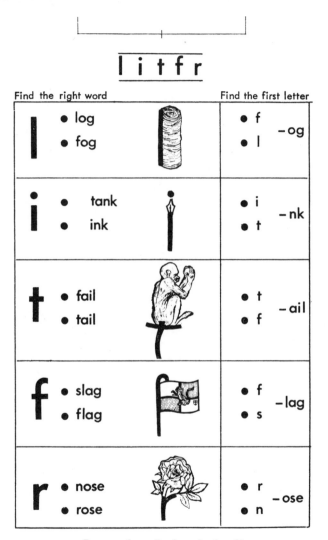

l i t f r

Find the right word		Find the first letter
l • log • fog		• f • l – og
i • tank • ink		• i • t – nk
t • fail • tail		• t • f – ail
f • slag • flag		• f • s – lag
r • nose • rose		• r • n – ose

Page 1 from Book 1 (reduced)

4. In Book 3, there is confusion with the unvoiced 'th' sound and the voiced 'th' sound. For example:

'Find the word with the same sound as *th*ree.'

A few of the correct responses are 'the', 'then', 'that'. It is emphasised that neither the books nor the Stillitron can have any success without the *full participation and guidance of the teacher throughout.*

5. The *Programmed Remedial Reading Texts* are a good attempt at providing an aid to reading which gives the child an immediate answer to his response. I have found that they are particularly useful for the older junior and the secondary child. The best results I have obtained have been with adult non-readers. These have benefited quite appreciably from this approach.

Stillit Books Ltd. has also published *Word-Control Remedial Readers*[1] for use with the Stillitron. They are for children of seven to twelve years of age who are ready for reading. Such children may be able to recognise a few words and copy quite accurately. It consists of graded reading material with instantaneous feedback. New material is introduced slowly and includes much repetition. Each package consists of four-page folders and has a distinct advantage over the books used in the *Programmed Remedial Reading Texts*. There are six series each consisting of eight folders with a test at the end of each series. The *Word-Control Remedial Readers* also provide the child with the opportunity of writing down the words and sentences in his exercise book.

(v) THE TAPE RECORDER

Of all the various teaching aids available to the teacher, probably none offers him more opportunities than the tape recorder. This device is considered by many to be the most

[1] Marshall, A. E., *Word-Control Remedial Readers,* Stillit Books Ltd., London, 1969.

versatile teaching aid developed in this generation.[1, 2] There are many models with such simple operation controls that almost anyone, even many infant children, may learn to use them successfully. The tape recorder may open up new avenues and help to create the stimulation which may have been difficult to provide in other ways.

I would suggest that the value of a tape recorder depends upon the skill and observations of the teacher who uses it and who recognises its limitations as well as its possibilities.

I have experimented with the use of the tape recorder as a reading aid for several years and accounts of this experimentation have been published in several journals.[3, 4, 5, 6]

Regardless of the success of the various methods used in the teaching of reading, we are still left with the problem of the effect of failure on the part of some of our pupils. The majority of non-readers and backward readers in our primary schools are late starters or slow learners whose difficulties may be so easily overlooked or not understood by the teacher who is attempting to teach large numbers covering the whole range of ability.

We are all well aware that when readiness for reading has been reached, 'beginning reading' should produce that initial success which will engender further success. Slow readers require adequate preparation before being confronted with their first books. It is at this stage that the slow or reluctant reader needs the maximum of individual attention. With

[1] Jones, J. G., *Teaching with Tape*, The Focal Press, London, 1962.

[2] Weston, J., *The Tape Recorder in the Classroom*, National Committee for Audio-Visual Aids in Education, 33 Queen Anne St., London, W.1., 1968.

[3] Hughes, J. M., 'Look, hear and say', *Forward Trends*, **10**, 1, 29–32, 1966.

[4] Hughes, J. M., 'Taped lessons to aid teaching of reading', *Teacher in Wales*, **8**, 16, 1–2, 1968 and **8**, 17, 15–16, 1968.

[5] Hughes, J. M., 'The tape recorder as a reading aid', *Teachers World*, 15 August, 1969.

[6] Hughes, J. M., 'Learning to read with the tape recorder', *Ways and Means*, Times Educ. Supp. 23 May, 1969.

staff/pupil ratios as they are at present, the problem appears to many as almost insurmountable.

In the normal classroom situation, the child must be left some time before the results of his reading efforts are confirmed. Frequently, the classroom situation is such that the slow readers are huddled together stammering over their primers and making innumerable visits to their teacher. This situation reinforces the sense of failure and offers little in the way of finding pleasure and meaning in reading.

How can a teacher give individual attention to one child and yet ensure that the other children are being taught? What teaching programme can children follow which involves a reading situation whereby they learn to read by reading? How can children learn to read and be assisted in their reading in the same way as they would if they were taught on a one to one basis?

In the early years I attempted to answer the above questions by experimenting with an old tape recorder and three pairs of army surplus headphones. The army headphones were eventually replaced by the Primary Audio Set[1] (Fig. 5). This set consists of a metal box which is plugged into the speaker or output extension of the tape recorder. The box serves as a volume booster and has six connections to which six stethoscope type headphones are easily attached.

Preparing the Taped Lessons

In the early stages of this work, I used my own material, but this eventually gave way to the use of published reading schemes and my own supplementary materials. The first reading scheme used was the *Ladybird Key Words Reading Scheme*[2]

[1] The Primary Audio Set, Code No. 20 c 204, S. G. Brown Ltd., King George's Avenue, Watford, Hertfordshire.

[2] Wills & Hepworth have recorded the first six reading books, 'a' series, each on separate tapes. *Ladybird Key Words Reading Scheme* by W. Murray. Wills & Hepworth, Loughborough.

and this was later followed by the *Oxford Colour Reading Books*[1].

I had previously used these reading schemes with my remedial groups and I was in a position to make a list of the 'sticking points' and other difficulties encountered by children. This list was to become very important when the lessons were being recorded and additional stress was placed on the 'sticking points'.

For some time before recording the taped lessons, I sat with my pupils and surreptitiously recorded the approach which I adopted when helping a child to read. I wanted the taped lessons to be as authentic as possible.

I found that the taped lessons should not be so fast that the slower reader is left behind nor so slow that they lose their impetus. I had to find the required speed as a result of experimentation with the use of a stop-watch. I discovered that if written responses are eventually required, it is wise to limit these to one word answers or the ringing and underlining of words. I had to ensure that the lessons were not too passive. The child must be involved throughout the lesson. This may be done by asking questions throughout the 'looking', 'listening' and 'reading' rather than leaving all the questions to the end.

I have found it useful to number the lines on each page so that the child may easily find the word to which the teacher wishes to refer.

Throughout the lesson the child is asked to read with the 'voice', read on his own, and point to words or sounds. For example:

> 'Point to the word "train".'
>
> 'Point to the word on the first line which begins with the sound "sh".'

The following is an outline of the approach which I have adopted with my taped reading lessons.

Part One: Pre-teaching Machine Activities

    Step 1. When a child begins to read his first book, he must

[1] *Oxford Colour Reading Books* by C. Carver & C. H. Stowasser, O.U.P.

experience success. Adequate preparation is required. This preparation involves the teaching of the first words that he will need when he receives his first recorded reading lesson. These activities involve the various word recognition games. Flash cards are used for word-word and word-picture matching exercises. Short sentences are made from the words contained in the first book and the child has practice at reading, writing and learning these sentences.

Part Two: The Beginning of Taped Reading Lessons

The use of the first books in the reading scheme. All books within each grade are of the same reading standard. Throughout the lessons, stress is placed on the 'sticking points'. Recording time is between 10 and 15 minutes.

Step 2. The children listen to the teacher's voice reading the story at normal speed. The voice tells them to look at the pictures and to turn over when told to do so.

Step 3. The children are told to turn back to the beginning of the story. This time the illustrations are studied once more and the children are asked to point to the words on the illustrations and read them aloud. A period of time is given, sufficient for the children to point and read. (The maximum period of time was found during the months of experimentation.) The voice asks the children whether they know the words.

'Read them once more with me.'

Step 4. When the last illustration has been discussed, the children are told to turn back to the beginning of the story.

'Now I want you to read the story with me. Remember to point to each word as you read it with me.'

The recording is quite slow, giving the child sufficient time to point to the word and vocalise.

Step 5. The next stage is for the teacher to listen to the child reading on his own. (Most children require two repetitions of the taped lesson before they are able to read unaided.)

Step 6. The next stage is for the child to complete the

F

various other activities involving further reading, writing, and other activities using the words already learned from reading the story.

Part Three: The Continuation of Taped Reading Lessons

Recordings of other books are introduced. The recording time is gradually extended from 10 to 15 minutes to 20 to 25 minutes. As the child progresses, and moves on through the reading scheme, the voice asks him to read more often, unaided. This approach is adopted more and more as the child becomes more proficient.

My work in this field is a reflection of the many experiments and work being carried out throughout the British Isles. Some first class work is being done at Pear Tree Spring Junior School, Stevenage[1]. At this school, a teaching laboratory has been built for as little as £30 as opposed to £750 plus if this had been installed by a commercial undertaking.

The Remedial Supply Company[2] is a company which has recently been formed to supply machines and taped requirements for all aspects of the teaching of reading.

Dr. R. I. Brown has developed *The Clifton Audio/Visual Reading Programme*[3] which is basically a phonic approach using taped materials, reading cards and workbooks.

The American '*Dialogue* 1'[4] is a programmed book to be used with tape-recordings.

A useful piece of equipment is a continuous loop tape cassette[5]. The tape is 200 feet long and fits all standard tape recorders without modification of any kind.

[1] *Ways and Means,* Times Educ. Supp., 22 March, 1968.

[2] The Remedial Supply Company, Dixon Street, Wolverhampton.

[3] *The Clifton Audio/Visual Reading Programme* by R. I. Brown & G. E. Bookbinder, ESA, Pinnacles, Harlow, Essex.

[4] 'Dialogue 1', *An Aural-Oral Course in Phonics* by A. Brogan & E. Hatchkiss. Chester Electronics Laboratories, Inc., Chester, Conn.

[5] Loop Tape Cassettes, King's, 105–107, Dawes Road, London, S.W.6

There are now single specially-designed tape recorders on which the pupil can copy a master recording which has been made on one track by recording it on a separate track of the same tape. The pupil can erase and re-record the lesson as often as he wishes without erasing the master recording on the other track. (This is the principle used in the language laboratory when learning a second or foreign language.) This facility has now been made available on the latest range of mains-operated tape recorders. (Philips EL3541H).

With the development of machines which allow children to create speech, it should be possible to accelerate the acquisition of reading skills and give the teacher more time to concentrate on those children who need her assistance.

(vi) FILMSTRIPS

For a number of years, teachers have been using filmstrips as a teaching aid in an attempt to awaken children's interest in books and to stimulate them to read for themselves.

Ideally, a teacher should read from a book and at the same time show the children the illustrations. But is this possible with a class of 36 or more children? Even if the teacher holds up the book, only a few children will be able to see the illustrations. However, when a filmstrip of the book's illustrations is used, the whole class becomes involved throughout the story.

There is a supply of filmstrips available for use with children who are at the early stages of reading, (see Appendix C), especially those produced for *The Happy Venture Reading Scheme*[1] with filmstrips for the Introductory Book and Books 1, 2, and 3. These filmstrips may be used very effectively with a teacher's live commentary or, what is sometimes more effective, a taped commentary.

The finest example which illustrates how filmstrips may awaken children's interest in books and stimulate them to read

[1] *The Happy Venture Reading Scheme* by F. J. Schonell. Oliver & Boyd, Edinburgh.

is provided by the excellent filmstrips produced by Weston Woods. These have been used in America for several years and arrived in this country in 1968. The approach adopted is quite simple and should stimulate many teachers in this country to adopt similar approaches of their own. The Weston Woods system is very effective, using the illustrations from outstanding picture books. The distributor in this country is the Children's Book Centre, 140 Church Street, Kensington, London, W.8.

The colour reproductions are excellent and the combination of narration and brilliantly illuminated pictures has a tremendous influence on young children, especially Sendak's strange tale 'Where the Wild Things Are'. The approach is to show the filmstrip to children and then give them the actual books to look at. I have no doubt that this form of story telling with 5 to 6 year-olds has a great value and the excellent pictures on the screen enrich children's experiences of books. I am sure that this approach will have a wider use in the future, especially with immigrant and culturally deprived children.

Morton Schindell, an American, is the inventor of these filmstrips. It was in 1955 that he began to produce films based on children's books. These films are made with the iconograph technique by which illustrations from books are photographed in such a way that there is the illusion of movement. A soundtrack of the text is synchronised with the pictures. From this work, Schindell began to concentrate on making filmstrips with a separate recorded reading of the text because he believed that there would be a greater demand for this approach.

There are booklets containing the text to help the storyteller. The filmstrip frames are reproduced down the margins of the booklets with an accompanying text.

It is not suggested that this approach should involve the abandonment of the traditional story-telling of the teacher. This approach, however, may supplement the usual form of story-telling with bright and colourful pictures on a screen or wall. This is a change from the teacher panning a story book containing a picture which cannot be seen by over half of the class. These filmstrips, therefore, awaken children's interest in books, and stimulate their desire to read for themselves with increased pleasure.

There are many teachers who are not enthusiastic about the use of filmstrips in this particular way because, they argue, the personal relationship between story teller and children no longer exists. It should be remembered, however, that the filmstrip is only a means of stimulating and encouraging children to read and that it is not forgotten that it is the book that really matters.

4

Other reading aids and media

A. The S.R.A. Reading Laboratories[1]

As a result of the abundance of knowledge arising from advances in technology over the last 20 years, more and more attention has been focused upon the methods, materials and devices used in the teaching of reading. Many new approaches and media have been designed to help the child read more easily. Teachers are focusing particular attention on the various materials which provide for the individual differences of children.

Reading development programmes are designed with the following points in mind:

1. Most children can improve on their present reading ability in the various reading skills.

2. Children who attempt material that is either too easy or too difficult will improve only very slightly.

3. A reading development programme should cater for the wide diversity of reading ability found in a typical class.

4. Opportunities should be provided for children to progress in reading skills as quickly and as far as their capacities will allow.

[1] The S.R.A. Reading Laboratories, Science Research Associates Ltd., Reading Road, Henley on Thames, Oxon.

Reading development programmes have the following aims:

1. To improve the child's skills of understanding reading and language, listening and speed of reading.

2. To provide reading material that gives regard to individual differences by allowing each child to begin at his own particular level and to proceed at his own particular rate.

3. To encourage independence and to develop powers of self-appraisal.

4. To include the reading development programme as an integral part of the overall reading programme in the class-room.

YEAR GROUP	NORMAL (wide ability range)	WELL ABOVE NORMAL (normal ability range)	VERY POOR	REMEDIAL (very retarded)
Top infants	Reading lab. 1a + word games	Reading lab. 1a + word games	———	———
1st year junior	Reading lab. 1b + word games	Reading lab. 1c + word games	Reading lab. 1a + word games	Word games
2nd year junior	Reading lab. 1c + word games	Reading lab. 2a	Reading lab. 1b + word games	1a + word games
3rd year junior	Reading lab. 2a	Reading lab. 2b	Reading lab. 1c + word games	1b + word games
4th year junior	Reading lab. 2b	Reading lab. 2c	Reading lab. 2a	1c + word games

EVENTUALLY TO READING LAB. 4a FOR 5TH AND 6TH SECONDARY GROUP.

Dr D. Parker designed the reading material for the S.R.A. Reading Laboratories (Figs. 6 and 7) with the requirements of American schools in mind. The ten reading laboratories are so designed that the children have a planned routine. The reading material is graded very carefully from a very elementary level to almost adult level. The reading laboratories are designed to meet the needs of children of varying ranges of ability in a given age group and to improve their reading skills of comprehension, vocabulary and speed. Two series are intended for the primary school and these are contained in six boxes (seven, if Reading Laboratory 1 : Word Games is used).

Most teachers fully appreciate that not all children of the same age will reach the stage of being able to read at the same time. This means that some children in the infant school and in first year juniors are still learning the basic decoding process while others are ready to utilize their recently acquired reading skills. The Reading Laboratory Series gives each child a course that is geared to his own ability level, and skills are acquired at the child's own rate of learning.

Initially, children are motivated by a series of interesting and colourful stories. These stories, however, have a male bias and it is unfortunate that girls are not catered for more fully. The series includes many interesting topics. The stories are naturally Americanized, but this is not a severe criticism of the material. The occasional Americanisms, (e.g. 'sidewalk', 'railroad', 'color' and 'pants' for 'trousers') and examples of the American way of life do not unduly perturb children.

The various levels within each reading laboratory are colour-coded so that when the child's reading ability has been ascertained and coded, he may work his way through the laboratory, marking and scoring his own work. The child scores and corrects the reading exercises himself and records the result on his own progress chart. These charts are useful in that they help the teacher to diagnose errors at an early stage.

Reading Laboratory 1 : Word Games is designed for use with

Reading Laboratories 1a, 1b, and 1c, but it is also very useful when used with any other reading scheme with a phonic basis. A Phonic Survey may be used by the teacher. The results of this Survey will show the child's strengths and weaknesses in phonics. The child may then be directed to those games which will provide him with the necessary exercises to overcome his weaknesses.

The 44 games contained in Reading Laboratory 1: Word Games cover 136 phonic and structural analysis skills and are played by pairs of children. Each child plays the word games listed on his programme and moves through these games at his own rate of learning.

Children are introduced to the work contained in the Reading Laboratories, i.e. 1a, 1b, etc., by means of a Listening Skill Builder. The teacher reads stories aloud from the Teacher's Handbook and then asks questions. The children choose their answers from a group given in their record books. They are able to check them and record their scores on progress charts in 'My Own Book for Listening'.

The Laboratories build comprehension and test vocabulary and word attack at all levels with brightly illustrated reading selections called Power Builders. The Power Builders consist of informative stories. Children record their times, answer several questions, check their answers, record their results as percentages and by graph and are able to make a daily assessment of their progress. A few teachers would probably regard this self-recording as a waste of time, but children become very adept at recording and the process adds to the child's involvement in his own progress.

Rate Builders are shorter reading passages. Because reading speed takes on more importance as pupils progress, the Laboratories, beginning with 2a, provide additional three minute exercises. The teacher signals the start and finish. Each of the exercises is followed by questions that determine how much the child has grasped. The child corrects his answers.

The S.R.A. Reading Laboratories are intended as a reading aid and not to replace other reading schemes or materials. They do, however, allow the teacher more time to help those in most need and act as a challenge to good readers who may tackle material at more difficult levels. It is interesting to note some of the conclusions of an investigation into the use of one of these Laboratories in three Midlothian schools by Pont[1]. It was concluded that the Reading Laboratory was really a 'crash' programme. It boosts a child's reading ability and enables him to reach his ceiling more quickly. It is very suitable for use in adjustment classes where the aim is to bring a child quickly up to a level at which he may again join his class.

The Laboratories are packed in boxes and the packaging is adequate for normal classroom use. The material is printed on good quality card and the illustrations are attractive. Due regard is paid to the developing visual abilities of children and the typography is of quite high quality. The teacher's manual is rather complicated, but an easier version is being prepared.

The cost may appear to be rather disturbing, but when it is appreciated that many children may use the material and that it covers such a wide range of age and ability then, I would suggest, it is a very sound investment.

Science Research Associates have also published BRS Satellites. This is a library for beginning readers. The Satellites consist of a collection of original stories and poems. The kit contains 380 four-page folders (two copies of each of 190 original selections) printed on strong cardboard. These selections are contained in a box and are divided into five graded levels with booklets for each level. The kit also includes a set of teacher's notes.

The SRA Pilot Libraries may be used with the SRA Reading Laboratory Series or they may be used on their own. Each library contains seventy-two books called Pilot Books and these

[1] Pont, H. B., 'An investigation into the use of the S.R.A. Reading Laboratory in three Midlothian schools.' *Educ. Res.*, **8**, 3, 230–236, 1966.

cover a large range of reading ages so that all the children in a class can find books at their own reading levels. Pilot Library 2A is suitable for the Junior School and 2B & 2C are suitable for Junior and Secondary Schools. 3B is suitable for the Secondary School.

I have no doubt that, in the future, there will be a growth of reading development programmes. In Australia, there is an equivalent reading development programme to the S.R.A. The Australian scheme is called WARDS (Western Australian Reading Development Scheme).

The Reading Workshop[1] has recently been published and this is specially designed for use by children in the 9 to 12 range. The Reading Workshop has three parts – Work Cards, Speed Cards and Answer Cards. Each part consists of 100 cards divided into 10 graded sections each containing 10 cards. Each section has a different colour and the sections are arranged in order of difficulty. The Brown section is the easiest and the Red the most difficult.

B. The Initial Teaching Alphabet (i.t.a.)[2]

It must be remembered that i.t.a. is not a method of teaching reading, but a medium. Indeed, teachers are advised to use the methods they have become accustomed to in teaching through the medium of traditional orthography (t.o.).

The alphabet in its original form was designed in 1837 by Isaac Pitman and was used in American Schools in a revised form under the title of 'Phonotopy' – printing by sound. Sir James Pitman redesigned this alphabet in the 1950's and it was introduced under the title of 'The Augmented Roman Alphabet'. The 44 characters used in printed texts are set out below. It will be noticed that 24 letters from our existing alphabet are retained and 20 new symbols are added.

[1] Reading Workshop. Ward Lock Educational Co. Ltd., 116 Baker Street, London, W1E 2EZ.

[2] The i.t.a. Foundation, 9 Southampton Place, London, W.C.1.

peeter woʃ sittiŋ bie himself. hee lʊkt pɔorly, and woʃ dresst in a red cotton pocket-haŋkerᴄhif.

"peeter,"—sed littl benjamin, in a whisper—"hɷ haʃ got yɷr clœᵵhʃ?"

From 'The Tale of Benjamin Bunny' by Beatrix Potter

a	ɑ	æ	aʋ	b	c	ch
apple	father	angel	author	bed	cat	chair

d	ɛɛ	e	f	g	h	ie
doll	eel	egg	finger	girl	hat	tie

i	j	k	l	m	n	ŋ
ink	jam	kitten	lion	man	nest	king

œ	o	ω	ꙍ	oʋ	oi	p
toe	on	book	food	out	oil	pig

r	ɼ	s	ʃh	ʒ	t	th
red	bird	soap	ship	treasure	tree	three

th	ue	u	v	w	wh	y
mother	due	up	van	window	wheel	yellow

z	ƨ
zoo	is

Some of the Main Features of i.t.a.

1. i.t.a. has only one print configuration for each English word, e.g. 'cat' and not Cat or CAT etc.

2. i.t.a. usually has only one symbol for each sound unit or phoneme. For example, ω is used for a variety of symbols used for this sound in traditional orthography, e.g. blue, too, through, shoe, fruit, zoo etc.

3. i.t.a. removes the irregularity of the relations between sound and printed symbols, e.g. 'o' as in 'one', 'bone', 'gone' etc. This is replaced by a coding which represents these different vowel sounds.

4. Where the two parts of the letter group are separated by another letter, this sound is represented by a single character, e.g. 'fine' – 'fien', 'hive' – 'hiev', 'ride' – 'ried'.

5. i.t.a. is designed to ease transition to t.o. As far as possible

the upper part of the i.t.a. configuration of whole words is similar to the upper part of t.o. configuration.

Sir James Pitman has claimed that children would learn to read more quickly, become more proficient and be able to transfer to traditional orthography without much difficulty. i.t.a. became the subject of wide research under the direction of the Reading Research Unit of London University Institute of Education in 1961. Unfortunately, experiments with i.t.a. had to cease in 1967 because of lack of funds. There is, however, an abundance of literature on the experiments carried out with i.t.a., especially those of Downing *et al.* [1, 2, 3, 4, 5, 6]

The first report in 1963 appeared to justify Pitman's claims, but recent reports, whilst they still favour children taught in i.t.a., do not show significant superiority of the i.t.a. children over the t.o. children in word recognition, speed or comprehension. The second experiment[7] had more rigorous experimental controls than the first one. Attempts were made to eliminate the effects of creating the feeling of being 'something special'. Publicity and visits were discouraged. (Southgate[8, 9] has emphasised the effects of 'reading drive' on i.t.a. results.)

[1] Downing, J. A., *The i.t.a. Reading Experiment.* Evans, London, 1964.

[2] Downing, J. A., *The Initial Teaching Alphabet Explained and Illustrated.* Cassell, London, 1964.

[3] Downing, J. A., *The i.t.a. Symposium.* N.F.E.R., London, 1966.

[4] Cartwright, D. & Jones, B., 'Further evidence relevant to the assessment of i.t.a.' *Educ. Res.*, **10**, 1, 65–71, 1967.

[5] Downing, J. & Jones, B., 'Some problems of evaluating i.t.a.: A second experiment.' *Educ. Res.*, **8**, 2, 100–114, 1966.

[6] Downing, J., Fyfe, T. & Lyon, M., 'The effects of the initial teaching alphabet (i.t.a.) on young children's written composition.' *Educ. Res.*, **9**, 2, 137–144, 1967.

[7] Downing, J. A., *The i.t.a. Symposium.* N.F.E.R., London, 1966.

[8] Southgate, V., 'Approaching i.t.a. with caution.' *Educ. Res.*, **7**, 2, 83–96, 1965.

[9] Southgate, V., 'A few comments on "reading drive".' *Educ. Res.*, 9, 2, 145–146, 1967.

The second experiment provided findings supporting those of the first experiment in that (a) t.o. was found to be difficult for children in the initial stages of acquiring reading skills; (b) when the experimental classes were tested in i.t.a. they consistently did better than those children in the control classes who were tested, naturally, in t.o.; (c) difficulty was experienced by the experimental groups at the stage of transfer to t.o. and a setback in their reading progress was noticed. In the second experiment, however, when the tests were given to all children in t.o., all the results, with one exception (the Schonell Graded Word Reading Test at the end of the second year) showed t.o. classes to be slightly better than i.t.a. classes.

I have found that in the early stages of reading, word recognition in i.t.a. appears to be easier for the child. Children appear to learn to read at an earlier age and i.t.a. has given us all room for thought in our concept of reading readiness[1]. A child is more easily able to express his thoughts in writing using this medium. If the child knows the shape of his sounds, he can think of an idea and write it down. This of course may be done using traditional spelling, but in the early stages the writing may be meaningless to the teacher. When i.t.a. is used, more immediate contact is made between teacher and child. There is no need for the child to be restricted to those short words which he can spell, he is able to attempt longer ones. I have found, however, that some children experience some difficulty in writing several of the characters and this detracts from the value of the writing process, e.g. ꟼh, ŋ, ʃh.

I would also suggest that there is a danger that children reading fluently in i.t.a. may not comprehend many of the words because they are outside their experiences.

I have found that, in a few cases, children have been transferred to a junior school where there is no i.t.a. and these children have not reached the stage of transfer to t.o. A further

[1] Downing, J. A., 'Is a "Mental Age of Six" essential for reading readiness?' *Educ. Res.*, **6**, 16–28, 1963.

problem arises when a child moves to a different part of the country. Transfer from school to school, because of the demands of society, is becoming a growing concern and if a child has to experience different approaches and media in early reading teaching, then this may be very detrimental.

In my opinion, continued use of i.t.a., with some children who are slow readers, impedes transfer to t.o. and these slow readers are actually hindered rather then assisted in their reading. Downing, however, recommends that reading in i.t.a. should continue until the child is reading fluently.

The Inner London Education Authority[1] carried out an investigation with the aim to ascertain whether, and how, the use of i.t.a. would affect the early reading progress of children when taught in their normal, every-day school setting. It is interesting to note a few of the investigation's findings:

1. Children made an earlier start with their first readers using i.t.a. It was not, however, a massive swing to a much earlier start. There were wide differences between pupils and schools.

2. Children made quicker progress, as a whole, throughout their infant school careers and this was especially marked in the earlier stages. The third term results were relatively better than those at the 'leaver' level, when the gap between i.t.a. and t.o. schools was much narrower.

3. The transfer to t.o. appeared to require a re-adjustment and further development of reading skills even of those used in word recognition. The transfer was found to be a lengthy and gradual process. When the complete change to i.t.a. is made, the teacher needs to be conscious of the new demands made on the children and be prepared to *teach* the new elements. It is suggested that transfer probably involves a loss of reading efficiency, in the sense that not all words which would be read in i.t.a would be readable in t.o. However, it would appear that

[1] 'Report on the use of The Initial Teaching Alphabet in a sample of London Schools (1963–67).' I.L.E.A.

the t.o. levels reached whilst the child is reading i.t.a. may not be affected when the child changes his medium, even if he is one of the poorer readers.

In conclusion, it must be remembered that i.t.a. is a medium and not a new teaching method; good teaching is still required. Unfortunately, many over-enthusiastic supporters of i.t.a. regard it as an elixir which will cure all their pupils' reading ills. I would also suggest that the enthusiasm of the teacher for the medium is a factor which has influenced the results of the many experiments which have taken place. These experiments, however, have established that i.t.a. has several advantages, but far more searching work is required before it is decided that this medium should be used with all children. After all, even Downing stresses that teaching reading skills, as well as reading comprehension, must be continued into the junior school for approximately half the age group and he particularly stresses the very wide range of individual differences in i.t.a. and t.o. groups.

Probably the final word, to date, should go to Warburton and Southgate[1] who have carried out an independent evaluation of i.t.a. for the Schools Council. The evidence, collected from a variety of sources, comes out in favour of the use of i.t.a. Research indicated that in most schools, but not all, infants using i.t.a. have learnt to read earlier and faster than similar children using t.o. However, evidence suggests that after nearly three years of using i.t.a. the reading ability of the 't.o.' children is at the same level as those who began with i.t.a.

Teachers using i.t.a. found that their children had no difficulty in transferring to t.o. Researchers, however, found that some children experienced a setback in reading attainment after transition.

All the evidence in this independent evaluation suggested a need for more research into the early stages of learning to read and into methods of assessing early reading ability.

[1] Warburton, F. W. & Southgate, V. *i.t.a. An Independent Evaluation.* W. & R. Chambers & J. Murray, 1969.

C. The Use of Colour

Many educationists, appreciating that English spelling is frequently inadequate and ambiguous, have looked for new approaches which give children more phonetic assistance. Diacritical marks have been used to indicate that a vowel may either make the sound of its name, e.g. cāke, mīne, rōse or make a shorter sound, e.g. măt, sĭt, hŏt. This system fails, however, when the child attempts to read such words as water, tomb etc. In 1953, B. L. Needle introduced his AU-T-O-FL-E-X S-Y-S-T-E-M[1] with the dictum – 'first give them the phonic elements – then ask them to read'. Needle oversimplifies the problem by stating that his Autoflex System is built around the belief that if a pupil first masters the single letter phonetics with additional sounds for 'c', 'g', and 'y' plus an absolutely clear grasp of the difference between the names and sounds of the letters, goes on to master blended consonants, then follows a carefully controlled study of imphonic diagraphs etc., he will be equipped to analyse and synthesise 99% of written English.

Colour has been used in an attempt to simplify the medium for the initial stages of learning to read by identifying sounds by colours but keeping the traditional form of spelling. The first book to be printed entirely in colour was published in 1899. This was the first book in a series by Nellie Dale. In the Dale Readers, only three colours were used plus black:

> black for voiced consonants.
>
> blue for unvoiced consonants,
>
> red for vowels,
>
> yellow for silent letters.

The Dale Readers used colour coding to help children to speak rather than read and many children must have experienced boredom with the long and tedious preparatory training involved.

[1] Autoflex Publications, 274a Fratton Road, Portsmouth, Hants.

Since Nellie Dale's attempt, colour has been used as an aid to the recognition of the sound value of letters by several educationists including Moxon[1], Gattegno[2] and Jones[3].

(i) WORDS IN COLOUR

Dr Gattegno's *Words in Colour* is growing in popularity throughout the British Isles, but it is more widely used in Australia. There are many teachers who are extremely enthusiastic over the success they claim they have achieved. *Words in Colour* has not received intensive investigation by research workers and the results of limited research have not favoured this approach.[4, 5]

Gattegno's intention is to reduce written English to a fully phonetic language for teaching purposes but maintaining conventional spelling. He does this by analysing the language into its constituent sounds and then representing each sound by a colour. For example, the letter 'a' as used to represent several different sounds:

w*a*s, w*a*ter, m*a*t, h*a*re, c*a*ke, *a*bout etc.

To these, Gattegno gives different colours in order that they may be distinguished.

Over 40 colours are used and they are used on Fidel Charts which contain all the differing ways in which the sound is represented in English spelling. These colours are also used on the 21 wall charts which are used for teaching the whole class or groups of children. In the early stages, the materials consist of coloured chalks, a wooden pointer and a set of 21 wall charts on which are printed words to give examples of the many ways of writing the 48 sounds selected here as sufficient to cover writ-

[1] Moxon, C. A. V., *A Remedial Reading Method*. Methuen, London, 1962.

[2] Gattegno, C., *Words in Colour*. Educational Explorers, London, 1962.

[3] Jones, J. K., *Colour Story Reading*. Nelson, London, 1967.

[4] Lee, T. in Brown, A. L., *Reading: Current Research and Practice*. Chambers, London, 1967.

[5] Brimer, M. in Wall, W. D., *New Research in Education*. N.F.E.R., London, 1967.

ten English. On these wall charts, as on the Fidel Charts, letters are coloured consistently according to the sound which they represent for the words in which they appear. The colour system is not used in the books for this scheme, nor are they illustrated. There is no punctuation or capital letters.

The approach begins by teaching the five vowels only. A white 'a' is drawn on the blackboard and the teacher says, 'The white one (as in m*a*t) sounds "a" – what is it?' The children then repeat the sound every time the teacher taps the letter with the pointer. For example,

'a, aaa, aaaa, aaa'.

When letters are linked it represents a shortening of time, and pauses are shown by spaces between letters. The children are trained to respond to letters individually and in groups so that they are prepared for word and sentence reading.

The next step is to use 'u' as in 'up'. This is given a yellow colour. A further three vowel sounds are used in this way. Children continue to read material using these vowels as follows:

'aei, iou, aeiu, eiau'.

Gattegno calls this 'dictation', but it is very similar to a form of phonic drill.

The consonant 'p' (brown) is added (the brown one) and the children now join consonant and vowel. For example,

'ap,pa,ep,pe,op,po,ip,pi,up,pu'.

By adding 't' many words may be made. Each new sign (letter) is in a different colour and is called by its colour name but is given its sound.

'pat, pet, pit, pot, pup, pip, pop, tip, top, tit' etc.

Children are encouraged to use as many combinations of letters as possible and then to separate the words from the nonsense words. For example,

'ut, it, et, ot, tap, tip, tut, tet' etc.

By adding three more signs (letters), many English words and sentences may be made:

'pat stops spot.' 'pup trips pat.'

Those words written on the blackboard are recognised on the second of the wall charts and are joined together with the pointer to make sentences and, later, stories.

Gattegno maintains that, with no help from the teacher, the children are free to use their own powers using shape, colour, position on the chart, or a key word, as guides to sound with no complete reliance on any one of these factors, because in practice, writing and reading develop step by step.

Many teachers have ignored the use of *Words in Colour* for several reasons. First, they are critical of Gattegno's claims for the speed and fluency which can be achieved by children using his approach. Secondly, they disagree with the form of phonic drill involved in this approach even though Gattegno suggests that children enjoy it and it does not interfere with intelligent reading at a later date. Personally, I have reached the conclusion that phonic drill may be very beneficial with certain children. Thirdly, many teachers suggest that this approach interferes with visual discrimination because it is a fact that some colours stand out far more than others. Finally, there is concern by many teachers that colour-blind children will fail to discriminate between colours. Although *Words in Colour* uses many colours and different tones of colour, the actual tones are far less important to the learner than his ability to see a specific difference between colours.

I would suggest that *Words in Colour* may be useful in the early stages of reading by helping sound and visual recognition of individual symbols. Furthermore, it has a very important attribute in that consonants are given no sounds of their own, but are only shown to sound with vowels. This, therefore, greatly diminishes the problem of blending.

Books and Materials for Words in Colour
The Cuisenaire Co., Ltd., 40 Silver Street, Reading, Berks.

1. *Wallcharts*. There are 21 coloured wallcharts containing

the colour code which shows how English may be transformed into a phonetic language of 48 separate sounds.

2. *The Fidel Chart.* The chart displays the colour symbols.

3. *The Teacher's Guide* and *Background Book.*

These are books on the theory and practice of *Words in Colour.*

4. *Primer Books.* These are printed in black and white and are related to the Fidel Chart and Wallcharts.

5. *Word Building Book.* This is in black and white and is intended for pupils' reference purposes.

6. *Worksheets.* There are two sets of seven. These offer opportunities for individual learning through reading games.

7. *Book of Stories.* This book contains 40 progressive stories.

(ii) COLOUR STORY READING

J. K. Jones, the author of *Colour Story Reading*, conducted investigations into visual perception in children[1]. The results of tests involving discrimination of words, shapes or letters showed that children obtained far higher scores when tested with material in colour than when tested with similar material in black print. It was suggested that one reason for this is that words contain far more information and clues to their identity when they are written in colour. These early investigations were followed by a series of experiments using *Colour Story Reading* in schools, involving hundreds of children of varying ages and abilities. The results were favourable and this research was eventually continued under the aegis of the Reading Research Institute of the University of London Institute of Education. The research results were published in 1967[2].

Colour Story Reading was designed to give complete consistency and reliability to the phonetic clues in black print by using three colours, red, blue and green – plus black, and to

[1] Jones, J. K., 'Colour as an aid to visual perception in early reading.' *Brit. J. Educ. Psychol.*, **35**, 1, 21–27, 1965.

[2] Jones, J. K., *Research Report on Colour Story Reading*. Nelson, London, 1967.

could cough country course

do shoe too true two through

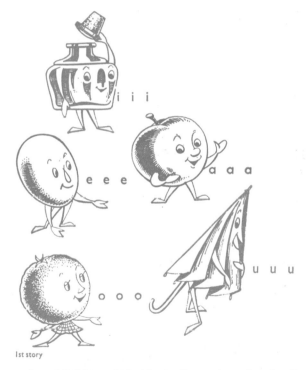

1st story

Page 2 from Mr Nen and his friends, Part 1 (greatly reduced)

present a learning situation which would help children to acquire basic reading skills for themselves.

The traditional spelling of English is retained and there is no change in the shape of letters. A wallchart displaying the colour symbol code is used but, in contrast to *Words in Colour*, the scheme is not based on wallcharts. The basis of the scheme is the use of reading books.

This scheme uses colour with the letters of the English alphabet but this use of colour is consistent and meaningful. For example, '*could*', '*cough*', '*country*', '*course*' and '*county*' all begin with the same three letters but are all pronounced in different ways. 'D*o*', 'sh*oe*', 't*oo*', 'tr*ue*', 't*wo*' and 'thr*ough*' all end with the same sound but all have different spellings. In *Colour Story Reading*, colour is used in the above examples to give the traditional letters complete consistency and reliability.

There are nine coloured backgrounds representing sounds, except for the blue circle which represents 'silence'. Three backgrounds are blue, three are red and three are green. Each background is square, triangular or circular. Letters are printed in black on these backgrounds.

The colour symbol code displayed on the wallchart contains 53 colour symbols representing 42 sounds and silent letters. A wide phonetic coverage has been achieved by using only three colours plus black. Those letters which cannot be accurately coded in colour are printed in black. Many of these black letters are regular.

'The Nineteen Stories' contain a close relationship between what happens in the stories and the sounds of the coloured words. For example, in one story an egg says 'eeeee'. An illustration in the children's books shows a green letter 'e' repeated three times by 'Egg'. These 'Nineteen Stories' describe the adventures of Mr Nen and his friends. The friends are Apple, Egg, Ink, Orange and Umbrella, and they talk by making the sounds of the short vowels.

All these stories are read to the children so that they

remember the situations, the characters and the sounds and when they look at their coloured reading books, 'Mr. Nen and His Friends', they use the previously read stories to connect the sounds with the printed symbols.

Even though *Colour Story Reading* is phonetic, it is recommended that the initial approach with this scheme should be by 'look and say', 'whole word' or 'sentence' methods. This has been suggested because it gives the children opportunities to discover and use phonetic cues for themselves. Another reason given is that a 'look and say' approach provides an opportunity for colour to supply additional visual information for the visual recognition of words and sentences.

Colour Story Reading is a scheme which teachers may find helpful but, as with *Words in Colour*, the colour symbol code should be regarded as a temporary prop to be dropped once the child is reading fluently. I have found that it has one important attribute in that the use of the colour symbol code encourages children to read words from left to right.

Books and Materials for Colour Story Reading
Thomas Nelson & Sons, Ltd., 36 Park Street, London, W.1.

1. *The Nineteen Stories*. This is a book for teachers' use. 42 individual sounds are introduced in a programmed sequence.

2. *The Discs*. There are three 12″ LP double-sided discs on which the stories have been recorded.

3. *Mr. Nen and His Friends*. These are three illustrated books printed in four colours.

4. *The Wallchart*. This displays 35 coloured letters, 9 digraphs and 9 coloured backgrounds making up the colour symbol code.

5. *The Teacher's Manual*. This gives a guide to the whole scheme.

Conclusions

The most valuable contribution to the teaching of reading is made when the teacher is in a position to give individual attention to the child. Teaching machines, tape recorders and other aids and media may cater to some extent for certain individuals, but they cannot replace the one to one approach of the teacher and the encouragement or support he is able to give.

It is at the beginning stage of reading that this personal contact is so very important. Eventually, when the child's reading ability increases, personal contact will become less, but the child should not be neglected at the beginning stage and the teacher must make every effort to hear children reading as often as possible. This is the finest teaching situation when the crux of the child's reading problem may be fully appreciated. Moyle[1] enumerates the values of hearing children read as follows:

'1. The child usually enjoys having the teacher's full attention centred upon him for a few moments and this increases effort on his part.

2. The teacher can impart a feeling of success which the child may not experience when reading on his own.

[1] Moyle, D., *The Teaching of Reading*. Ward Lock Educational, London, 1968 p. 118.

3. The child can be helped to bring expression into his reading.

4. New words met can be discussed and added to the child's vocabulary.

5. The teacher can observe the progress being made by the child and therefore can follow up the sessions by providing materials which will promote reading growth.

6. The teacher will note any difficulties being experienced and thus be able to devise activities to remedy them.

7. The teacher can keep a constant check on the child's understanding of what is read.'

Ideally, the teacher should listen to children reading every day, but it is fully appreciated that this is impossible with a class of between 30 and 40 children. Even when a teacher attempts to listen to as many children as she can, she is naturally concerned about what the other children are doing. It is in this situation that the various suggestions in *Aids to Reading* will be useful. Games and activities, self-corrective materials, workbooks, teaching machines and other aids and media may be used to supplement the teacher's individual contact. This would also give the teacher the opportunity to attend to the poor reader who requires more personal attention.

As a result of continued research in reading and related disciplines, combined with new insights into the interests of individual children, gradual changes are taking place in approach, materials and media. I appreciate the importance of innovations in the teaching of reading, but there appears no doubt that the teacher is still one of the most powerful forces in the actual teaching. Various investigations into the effectiveness of various methods, aids and materials frequently reveal significant differences in the effectiveness of their use, with the teacher frequently making the significant difference. It would be very interesting to read the results of investigations into the characteristics of teachers which are most conducive to pupils' reading progress.

The order in which various reading skills are introduced and the ways in which mastery of these skills can best be assisted have been highlighted as new approaches to programmed learning have been introduced. For instance, several examples of programmed reading material have adopted the sequence of teaching word recognition first and the teaching of phonics later, yet others teach phonics first. But there is still much research to be carried out in order to determine the most effective sequences to adopt for teaching reading. Then there is the problem of deciding which sequences within a sequence should be used. Should the teaching of consonant sounds precede that of vowels? Should children be taught to understand details before comprehension?

I have no doubt that teachers are more successful in the teaching of reading if they are convinced of the value of their own approach and are allowed to carry it out. A teacher with a strong preference for a particular approach may become far less effective if forced to conform to a completely new approach. I also have no doubt that many teachers need guidance in the use of methods, apparatus and other aids and media. Teaching Material Centres, as discussed by Williams[1] would be of tremendous benefit to many teachers.

We are continually searching for new methods of teaching reading and new materials and aids for this teaching, but it must be remembered that the way they are used is the key to success. McCullough[2] describes the situation as follows:

'The lesson of history (including the history of reading programs) seems clear. To accept one embodiment of an idea as

[1] Williams, P., 'A materials centre for special education', *Educ. Res.* **9**, 1, 53–55, 1966.

[2] McCullough, C. M. in Robinson, H. M. (Ed.), *Innovation and Change in Reading Instruction*, The National Society for the Study of Education, Chicago, Illinois, 1968. p. 355.

the best expression of it may do the idea a disservice. To accept one embodiment of a "new" idea as a suitable substitute for all that other programs offer is probably to mistake a new part for the whole and to invite a harmful imbalance. Blind men who have felt a part of the elephant are certain of the value of their discoveries; but if they are concerned with truth, they will have to admit the possible value of the discoveries of others. What if they tried to put this elephant together?'

Appendix A: A selection of teaching machines used in the teaching of reading

1. **The Canterbury Mk. II Teaching Machine.**
   E.S.A., Pinnacles, Harlow, Essex.
2. **The Esatutor.**
   E.S.A., Pinnacles, Harlow, Essex.
3. **The Language Master.**
   Bell & Howell, Alperton House, Bridgewater Road,
   Wembley, Middlesex.
4. **The Language Master Model 701.**
   Bell & Howell, Alperton House, Bridgewater Road,
   Wembley, Middlesex.
5. **The Stillitron.**
   Stillit Books Ltd.,
   72 New Bond Street, London, W.1.
6. **The New Craig Reader.**
   I.T.M. Ltd., Ashford, Middlesex.
7. **The Bristol Tutor.**
   E. J. Arnold, Butterley Street, Leeds.
8. **The Bingley Tutor.**
   E. J. Arnold, Butterley Street, Leeds.
9. **Individual Progressor.**
   R. H. L. Arnold, 14 Granville Road, Sheerness, Kent.
10. **I.T.M. Grundymaster.**
    I.T.M. Ltd., Ashford, Middlesex.

11. **The Readmaster AVO12.**
    E. J. Arnold, Butterley Street, Leeds.
12. **The Synchrofax Recorder AV007.**
    E. J. Arnold, Butterley Street, Leeds.
13. **The Talking Page.**
    Rank–REC Ltd.,
    11 Belgrave Road, London, S.W.1.

Appendix B: A selection of reading schemes

What to look for in a Reading Scheme.

1. The colour illustrations and story content should be so designed to attract and interest the reader. The illustrations should be bold, clear and coloured.

2. The scheme should, as far as possible, reflect the natural interests and activities of children and help to create a desirable attitude towards learning.

3. The books should have brightly coloured covers; they should be durable and well bound and, preferably, not larger than Quarto size.

4. The first books should offer relatively quick success in order to give further encouragement to children.

5. The type should be bold, clear and constant. The length of the line should be short with not too many words on each page.

6. The scheme should be carefully graded with adequate repetition of words and a repetition of such words in different contexts. Preferably, the vocabulary should be made up from a Basic Word List.

7. It should contain words that would be used frequently in the natural conversation of children and in their written work.

8. The steps between one book and the next should be gradual.

9. The framework for teaching phonics should be incidentally built into the scheme.

Pre-reading Books

1. *Are You Ready?* Macmillan.
2. *Getting Ready for Reading.* Ginn.
3. *Macmillan's Picture Books.* Macmillan.
4. *Bluebird Scheme.* Chambers.
5. *Kenny Books.* Philip & Tacey.
6. *Ladybird Learning to Read Books.* Wills & Hepworth.

Reading Schemes for Infants

1. *Ladybird Key Words Reading Scheme.* Wills & Hepworth.
2. *The Queensway Reading Scheme.* Evans.
3. *Ready to Read Scheme.* Methuen.
4. *Let's Learn to Read.* Blackie.
5. *McKee Readers* and *Platform Readers.* Nelson.
6. *Bluebird Scheme.* Chambers.

Reading Books with a Phonic Bias

1. *Sound Sense.* E. J. Arnold.
2. *Learn Your Sounds.* Blackie.
3. *Sounds and Words.* U.L.P.
4. *Royal Road Readers.* Chatto & Windus.
5. *Gay Way Reading Scheme.* Macmillan.
6. *Sounding and Blending.* Gibson.

Further Suggestions

1. *Beginning to Read Books.* Ernest Benn. (12 books.)
   Reading Age: 6–7 years. Interest Age: 7–10 years.
2. *Cowboy Sam Series.* E. J. Arnold. (9 books.)
   Reading Age: 6–8 years. Interest Age: 7–11 years.
3. *The Go Readers.* Blond. (4 Books.)
   Reading Age: 6–7½ years. Interest Age: 9–13 years.
4. *The Griffin Readers.* E. J. Arnold. (12 books.)
   Reading Age: 6–8 years. Interest Age: 8–14 years.
5. *Mike and Mandy Readers.* Nelson. (12 books.)
   Reading Age: 6–8½ years. Interest Age: 8–12 years.

6. *Ladybird Key Words Reading Scheme*. Wills & Hepworth. (36 books.)
   Reading Age: 5–9 years. Interest Age: 5–11 years.
7. *Oxford Colour Readers*. O.U.P. (30 books.)
   Reading Age: 6–9 years. Interest Age: 8–13 years.
8. *Racing to Read*. E. J. Arnold. (16 books.)
   Reading Age: 5–7½ years. Interest Age: 7–11 years.
9. *Sea Hawk Series*. E. J. Arnold. (8 books.)
   Reading Age: 6–8 years. Interest Age: 10+ years.
10. *Burgess Readers*. U.L.P. 4 books.
   Reading Age: 8–9½ years. Interest Age: 10+ years.
11. *Far and Near Books*. Chambers. (26 books.)
   Reading Age: 7–9 years. Interest Age: 9–15 years.
12. *True Adventure Series*. Blackie. (32 books.)
   Reading Age: 8 years. Interest Age: 9–15 years.
13. *Bandit Books*. Ernest Benn. (8 books.)
   Reading Age: 9+ years. Interest Age: 10–15 years.
14. *Jet Books*. Cape. (6 books.)
   Reading Age: 9+ years. Interest Age: 11–15 years.
15. *Tempo Books*. Longmans. (10 books.)
   Reading Age: 6½–8½ years. Interest Age: 9–13 years.
16. *Windrush Books*. O.U.P. (8 books.)
   Reading Age: 9+ years. Interest Age: 10–13 years.
17. *Spotlight on Trouble Series*. Methuen
   Reading Age: 8–10 years. Interest Age: 11–14 years.
18. *Working World Series*. Cassell. (5 books.)
   For slow readers in the secondary school.
19. *Teenage Twelve*. Gibson. (12 books.)
   Reading Age: 7+ years. Interest Age: 9–13 years.
20. *Swift Readers*. Harrap.
   Reading Age: 7–11 years. Interest Age: 9–14 years.

Appendix C: A selection of commercially produced reading materials

1. *Materials Supplied by Philip & Tacey Ltd., 69-79 Fulham High Street, London, S.W.6.*
Chelsea Alphabet Chart and Pictorial Symbols.
Chelsea Alphabet Cellograph Symbols.
Groundwork Key Words and Pictures.
Groundwork Key Word Coloured Gummed Stamps.
Renown Individual Picture and Word Matching Cards.
My Phonogram Workbooks.
My Books of Word Families.
Polly Strip Reading Books.
Family Cellograph Materials.
Chameleon Street Cellograph Picture Making Outfit.
People Who Work for Us Jig Saw Puzzles.

2. *Materials Supplied by Thomas Hope & Sankey Hudson Ltd., 123 Pollard Street, Manchester, 4.*
Child Guidance Magnetic Alphabet Boards.
Scrabble for Juniors.
Scrabble. (Full-size word-building game.)

3. *Materials Supplied by Education Supply Assoc. Ltd., Pinnacles, Harlow, Essex.*
ESA Picture Lotto.

Flannelgraph Crossword.
Card Picture Dominoes.
ESA Jig Saws. (Printed on wood.)

4. *Materials Supplied by E. J. Arnold & Son Ltd., Butterley Street, Leeds.*
Snappy Snap.
Shape Sorting.
Picture Word Charts.
Spellmaster.
Photo Puzzles.

5. *Materials Supplied by Robert Gibson & Sons Ltd., 2 West Regent Street, Glasgow, C.2.*
Word Games
Tear-off Picture and Word Pads.
Sounding and Blending. (5 books)
Sounds Right. (3 books)
My Pets.
My Home.
My School.
My Toys.

6. *Materials Supplied by the Remedial Supply Company, Dixon Street, Wolverhampton.*
Familiar Situations.
Stories Without Words.
Action Pictures.
Stories Without Words – The Parables.
The Reading Cards.
Tapes with Work Material.

7. *Materials Supplied by James Galt & Co., Ltd., Brookfield Road, Cheadle, Cheshire.*
Phonic Word Jig Saws.

Rhymo.
Picture Word Lotto.
Junior Scrabble.
Phonic Self Teacher.
Key Words Self Teaching Cards.
Phonic Practice Cards.
Self Checking Phonic Alphabet.
Double Dominoes. (Picture and word.)
Find-a-Pair.
Early Reading Jig Saws.
Flannelgraph Phonic Reading Set.
Flannelgraph Backcloth.

8. *Filmstrips by Weston Woods. Supplied by Children's Book Centre, Church Street, Kensington, London.*
Where the Wild Things Are.
Zozo Rides a Bike.
The Tale of Peter Rabbit.

9. *Filmstrips Supplied by Foundation Film Library, Brooklands House, Weybridge, Surrey.*
Alphabet. (Colour. 26 frames.)
What Shall We Do? (Black & white. 30 frames. 7 years and under.)
What Is It? (Black & white. 30 frames. 7 years and under.)
Tell Me About It. (Black & white. 25 frames. 7 years and under.)
Let's Make a Train. (Black & white. 44 frames. 5–7 years.)
Jeremy's Day. (Black & white. 29 frames. 5–7 years.)
David and Jane on the Farm. (Black & white. 34 frames. 5–7 years.)
Fat Pig. (Black & white. 40 frames 5–7 years.)
Snowman. (Black & white. 41 frames. 5–7 years.)
Tom and his Kite. (Black & white. 21 frames. 5–7 years.)
The Happy Venture Readers. (Strips for Introductory Book

and Books 1, 2, 3, 4. About 100 frames for each strip. 5–7 years.)

10. *Published by Ward Lock Educational, 116 Baker St, London, WIM 2BB.*

Reading Workshop (SBN 7062 35762).

11. *Published by Macdonald Educational, B.P.C. Publishing, 49/50 Poland St, London, W.1.*

Wordmaster Major (A group learning aid for basic language skills.)

Appendix D: Some common difficulties in reading and methods of treatment

1. *Reversals*
   i. Use exercises to emphasise the direction of reading such as tracing, pointing with the finger and underlining during reading.
   ii. Use a mask which shows one line of print at a time.
   iii. Use a sand tray.
   iv. Use specific training to aid the child in developing a sense of direction from side to side and up and down.
   v. Give the child exercises in joining dots in a set order.

2. *Mispronunciation – confusing similar consonants or vowels.*
   i. Speech training together with abundant practice in recognising letters seen and heard.
   ii. Provide the child with lists of words visually and orally.
   iii. Provide practice in the analysing of words.

3. *Guessing*
   i. Provide easier material.
   ii. Use word games in which phonic analysis is emphasised.
   iii. Enlarge the child's vocabulary by means of various kinds of activities.

4. *Additions and Omissions*
   i. Emphasise the meanings of words being read.

ii. Use cards with incomplete sentences and completed ones for comparison purposes.

iii. Ask the child to read with you.

5. *Omission of Lines*
   i. Provide material with wide line spacing.
  ii. Allow the child to use a ruler to underline while reading.
 iii. Use a mask which reveals one line at a time.

6. *Staccato Reading*
   Use flash cards containing phrases or sentences which demand an action response from the child so that he shows that he understands the meaning.

7. *Poor Interpretation*
   i. Provide easier material.
  ii. Use flash cards containing sentences in order to emphasise meaning.
 iii. Provide the child with material which caters for his interest and thus provide a motive for reading.

8. *Inability to Appreciate Details in a Description*
   i. Provide easier materials and completion exercises.
  ii. Ask the child to underline correct answers.

Appendix E: A suggested order for teaching phonics

1. Initial, Single Consonants (i)
   t, b, n, r, m, s, d, c (hard as in *cat*), *p, g* (hard as in *goat*)
2. Short Vowels
   (i) Initial Sounds
       a as in *apple*
       i as in *ink*
       e as in *elephant*
       o as in *orange*
       u as in *umbrella*.
   (ii) Middle Sounds
       a as in *bat*
       i as in *tin*
       e as in *pet*
       o as in *hot*
       u as in *jug*.
   (iii) *y* in different positions as in *yes, baby, fly*.
3. Initial, Single Consonants (ii)
   f, l, v, h, w, k, j, z.
4. Double Consonants
   bb, dd, ff, gg, etc. (including *ck*)
   Two identical consonants together make the same sound as one.

5. Initial Consonant Digraphs
   ch, sh, th (as in *three*), *wh, th* (as in *there*), *qu.*
6. Initial Consonant Blends
   st, sp, sc, sk, sl, sm, sn, sw, br, cr, dr, fr, pr, gr, tr, bl, pl, cl, fl, gl.
7. Vowel Digraphs
   ai, ay, oi, oo (two sounds as in *wood* and *fool).*
   oa, ow, ou (also has *ow* sound).
   au, aw, al, ee, ea (two sounds as in *bean* and *head*).
8. Other Sounds for *c, g, s*
   c followed by *e, i* or *y* has a soft (*s*) sound.
   g followed by *e, i* or *y* has a soft (*j*) sound.
   s makes the (*z*) sound as in *has.*
9. The Final and Silent *e.*
   e at the end of a word:
   (i) Functionless role – as in *kettle, jungle, noise.*
   (ii) Modifying role – can make the preceding vowel long or short.
   (iii) Special pronunciation of *are* as in *fare, ire* as in *fire, ure* as in *pure.*
10. Modification of Vowels by *r.*
    A vowel followed by *r* often makes a new sound.
    ar as in *car, or* as in *for, er* as in *sister, ir* as in *girl, ur* as in *burn.*
    Modification by *w* as in *warm, worm.*

References

Bhattacharya, S. *Programmed Remedial Reading Texts.* Stillit Books, London, 1967.

Brimer, M. in **Wall, W. D.** *New Research in Education.* N.F.E.R., London, 1967.

Cartwright, D. and **Jones, B.** 'Further evidence relevant to the assessment of i.t.a.' *Educ. Res.,* **10**, 1, 65–71, 1967.

Cashdan, V. and **Pumfrey, P. D.** 'Some effects of the remedial teaching of reading.' *Educ. Res.,* **11**, 2, 138–142, 1969.

Chall, J. *Learning to Read.* McGraw-Hill, New York, 1967.

Collins, J. E. *The Effects of Remedial Education.* Oliver & Boyd, Edinburgh, 1961.

Cox, M. (Ed.) *The Challenge of Reading Failure.* N.F.E.R., London, 1968.

Curr, W. and **Gourlay, N.** 'The effects of practice on performance in scholastic tests.' *Brit. J. Educ. Psychol.,* **30**, 2, 155–167, 1960.

Diack, H. *Reading and the Psychology of Perception.* Ray Palmer, Nottingham, 1960.

Doman G. *Teach Your Baby to Read.* Cape, London, 1963.

Downing, J. A. 'Is a "Mental Age of Six" essential for reading readiness?' *Educ. Res.,* **6**, 16–28, 1963.

The i.t.a. Reading Experiment. Evans, London, 1964.

The Initial Teaching Alphabet Explained and Illustrated. Cassell, London, 1964.

The i.t.a. Symposium N.F.E.R., 1966

Downing, J. A. and **Jones, B.** 'Some problems of evaluating i.t.a. A second experiment.' *Educ. Res.*, **8**, 2, 100–114, 1966.

Downing, J., Fyfe, T. and **Lyon, M.** 'The effects of the initial teaching alphabet (i.t.a.) on young children's written composition.' *Educ. Res.*, **9**, 2, 137–144, 1967.

Gattegno, C. *Words in Colour*. Educational Explorers, London, 1962.

Goldsmith, M. (Ed.) *Mechanisation in the Classroom*. (An introduction to teaching machines and programmed learning.) Souvenir Press, London, 1963.

Goodacre, E. J. *Teaching Beginners to Read: Report No. 2. Teachers and their Pupils' Home Background*. N.F.E.R., 1967.

H.M.S.O. *Progress in Reading*, Educ. Pamph. No. 50, 1966.

H.M.S.O. *Children and their Primary Schools*. A Report of the Central Advisory Council for Education (England), 1967.

Hughes, J. M. 'Look, hear and say.' *Forward Trends*, **10**, 1, 29–32, 1966.

'Taped lessons to aid teaching of reading.' *Teacher in Wales*, **8**, 16, 1–2, 1968, and **8**, 17, 15–16, 1968.

'The tape recorder as a reading aid.' *Teachers World*, (15 August, 1969.)

'Learning to read with the tape recorder.' *Ways and Means*, Times Educ. Supp. 23 May 1969.

Inner London Education Authority *Report on the use of the Initial Teaching Alphabet in a sample of London Schools* (1963–67).

Jones, J. G. *Teaching with Tape*. Focal Press, London, 1962.

Jones, J. K. 'Colour as an aid to visual perception in early reading.' *Brit. J. Educ. Psychol.*, **35**, 1, 21–27, 1965.

Jones, J. K. *Colour Story Reading* (Teacher's Manual). Nelson, London, 1967.

Jones, J. K. *Research Report on Colour Story Reading*. Nelson, London, 1967.

Kay, H., Dodd, D. and **Sime, M.** *Teaching Machines and*

Programmed Instruction, Penguin Books Ltd., Harmondsworth, 1968.

Kellmer-Pringle, M. L. *11,000 Seven-Year Olds* Longmans, London, 1966.

Lee, T. in **Brown, A. L.** *Reading: Current Research and Practice.* Chambers, London, 1967.

Leedham, J. and **Unwin, D.** *Programmed Learning in the Schools.* Longmans, London, 1967.

Lovell, K., Johnson, E. and **Platts, B.** 'A summary of a study of the reading ages of children who had been given remedial teaching.' *Brit. J. Educ. Psychol.*, **32**, 66–67, 1962.

Lovell, K., Byrne, C. and **Richardson, B** 'A further study of the educational progress of children who had received remedial education.' *Brit. J. Educ. Psychol.*, **33**, 1, 3–9, 1963.

Malmquist, E. *Factors Related to Reading Disabilities in the First Grade of the Elementary School.* Almqvist & Wiksell, Stockholm, 1958.

McCullough C. M. in **Robinson, H. M.** (Ed.) *Innovation and Change in Reading Instruction.* The National Society for the Study of Education, Chicago, Illinois, 1968.

McNally, J. and **Murray, W.** *Key Words to Literacy.* Schoolmaster Publishing Co., Ltd., London, 1962.

Morris, J. M. *Standards and Progress in Reading.* N.F.E.R., London, 1966.

Moxon, C. A. V. *A Remedial Reading Method.* Methuen, London, 1962.

Moyle, D. *The Teaching of Reading.* Ward Lock Educational, London, 1968.

Neale, M. D. *Neale Analysis of Reading Ability.* Macmillan, London, 1958.

Pont, H. B. 'An investigation into the use of the SRA Reading Laboratory in three Midlothian schools.' *Educ. Res.*, **8**, 3, 230–236, 1966.

Romiszowski, A. J. *The Selection and Use of Teaching Aids.* Kogan Page, London, 1968.

Roucek, J. S. (Ed.) *Programmed Teaching.* (A symposium on automation in education.) Peter Owen, London, 1966.

Sampson, O. C. 'Reading skill at eight years in relation to speech and other factors.' *Brit J. Educ. Psychol.,* **32,** 12–17, 1962.

Schonell, F. J. *The Psychology and Teaching of Reading.* Oliver & Boyd, Edinburgh, 1961.

Southgate, V. 'Approaching i.t.a. results with caution.' *Educ. Res.,* **7,** 2, 83–96, 1965.
'A few comments on "reading drive".' *Educ. Res.,* **9,** 2, 145–146, 1967.

Stott, D. H. *Manual for the Programmed Reading Kit.* Holmes–McDougall, Edinburgh, 1962.

Stott, D. H. *Roads to Literacy.* Holmes–McDougall, Edinburgh, 1964.

Times Educ. Supp. *Ways and Means.* 22 March, 1968.

Warburton, F. W. and **Southgate, V.** *i.t.a. An Independent Evaluation,* W. & R. Chambers & J. Murray, 1969.

Weston, J. *The Tape Recorder in the Classroom.* National Committee for Audio-Visual Aids in Education, London, 1968.

Williams, P. 'A materials centre for special education.' *Educ. Res.,* **9,** 1, 53–55, 1966.

Suggestions for further reading

Ablewhite, R. C. *The Slow Reader.* Heinemann, London, 1967.

Bond, G. L., and **Wagner, E. B.** *Teaching the Child to Read.* Macmillan, New York, 1966.

Daniels, J. C. and **Diack, H.** *The Phonic Method of Teaching Reading.* Chatto & Windus, London, 1957.

Daniels, J. C. and **Diack, H.** *The Royal Road Readers.* Teacher's Handbook. Chatto & Windus, London, 1967.

Dean, J. *Reading, Writing and Talking,* Black, London, 1969.

Diack, H. *In Spite of the Alphabet.* Chatto & Windus, London, 1965.

Fries, C. C. *Linguistics and Reading.* Holt, Rinehart & Winston, London, 1963.

Glynn, D. M. *Teach Your Child to Read.* Pearson, London, 1964.

Goodacre, E. J. *Teaching Beginners to Read: Report No. 1. Reading in Infant Classes.* N.F.E.R., 1967.

Johnston, S. *Achieving Reading Success.* Cambridge Aids to Learning Ltd., 1969.

Jones, J. K. 'Comparing i.t.a. with colour story reading,' *Educ. Res.,* **10**, 3, 226–234, 1968.

Lamb, R. T. *Aids to Modern Teaching: A Short Survey.* Pitman, London, 1967.

Morris, R. *Success and Failure in Learning to Read.* Oldbourne, London, 1965.

Money, J. (Ed.) *Reading Disability, Progress and Research Needs in Dyslexia.* The Johns Hopkins Press, Baltimore, 1962.

Ray, M. *See What I Mean?* (Design and production of individual visual aids.) Cassell, London, 1953.

Roberts, G. R. *Reading in Primary Schools.* Routledge, 1969.

Roswell, F. and **Natchez, G.** *Reading Disability, Diagnosis and Treatment.* Basic Books, London, 1964.

Segal, S. S. *Teaching Backward Children.* Evans, London, 1963.

Stern, C. and **Gould, T. S.** *Children Discover Reading.* Harrap, London, 1966.

Tansley, A. E. *Reading and Remedial Reading.* Routledge, London, 1967.

Vernon, M. D. *Backward Readers.* The College of Special Education, London, 1968.

Webster, J. *Practical Reading. Some New Techniques.* Evans, London, 1965.